THE LITTLE BLACK BOOK OF COMPUTER

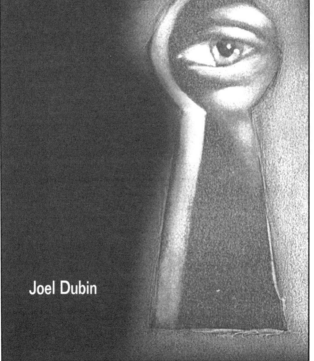

SECURITY

Joel Dubin

A Division of
Penton Technology Media
221 E. 29th Street • Loveland, CO 80538 USA
(800) 650-1804 • (970) 663-4700 • www.pentontech.com/education

29th Street Press® is a division of
Penton Technology Media
Loveland, Colorado USA

© 2005 by Joel Dubin
and Penton Media, Inc.

This book was printed and bound in Canada.

ISBN 1-58304-120-6

2007 2006 2005   WL   10 9 8 7 6 5 4 3 2 1

Las palabras que se diga al aire,
las paredes oyen.

To my dear wife, Sara,
for all her love and support
in my endeavors.

About the Author

Joel Dubin, CISSP, works as an independent computer-security consultant who is based out of Chicago. He has received multiple certifications from Sun Microsystems in the Java programming language as well as MBA and BA degrees from Northwestern University. He holds an Amateur Extra Class radio-operator license and maintains fluency in several foreign languages.

Table of Contents

CHAPTER 1

WHY READ THIS BOOK?

YOU'RE AN IT MANAGER OR A BUSINESS MANA-
ger who oversees IT operations, and your network is the heart of
your business. The network is what makes your business function —
it is your livelihood, in other words. Yet, unless you take ongoing
steps to protect it, your network is not safe.

Just as you lock the front door to your home and restrict the
number of people who receive a set of keys, you want to do the
same things for your network. However, countless companies leave
the doors to their networks wide open or give the keys away to all
of their employees. Typically, the people in charge aren't aware of
the potential for damage.

What would you do if the worst happened? If an intruder broke
into your home (you can imagine the results), you would probably
call the police. The officers would gather evidence, pursue the per-
petrator, and possibly recommend that you install a burglar alarm to
prevent future break-ins. The same course of action applies to your
network. You need to install an Intrusion Detection System, which
is the hi-tech equivalent of a burglar alarm, to detect network intruders. You also need a modus operandi for responding to the network
break-ins that can happen despite your best efforts.

What about the employees who must access the network for
their jobs? The company staff members are not your enemies — but
neither are they your friends. They are there to help the business

grow. You should set limits on the employees' stay just as you would for the guests in your home. You would not allow guests to carve their initials into your expensive oak furniture nor to trash your house. Correspondingly, you would not want a network user to intentionally download and store pornography nor to unintentionally download a worm that could take control of your entire system.

Why Is Pornography a Security Issue?

Pornography consists only of pictures, so what's the harm, right? Well, pornography can create security issues on two fronts: by damaging your system and by producing a source of legal liability. First, pornography is a less than wholesome business. This fact means that porn site operators are often less than careful about configuring their servers, which can then become magnets for viruses, spam, and other online hazards. These hazards can, in turn, damage your system; furthermore, downloaded pornography takes up precious storage space on your company servers. Second, most organizations have strict rules against sexual harassment and consider pornography as such. Not only does downloaded pornography thus create potential legal liability, but child pornography, of course, is just plain illegal.

Security calls for a balance of paranoia and practicality. The only truly safe computer is one that is turned off but, obviously, no computer user can live that way. Maintaining security requires a pattern of behavior and a mind-set. You cannot simply devise a one-shot plan which, although well conceived, is then stored on a bookshelf and forgotten until disaster strikes. Maintaining security is constant and ongoing — it is a way of life.

To that end, this book provides a comprehensive checklist that you can use to secure your network. Even if you have procedures for locking down your network that have succeeded until now, this book can help you check off others that you might have missed. And, although no system is ever completely secure, this checklist supplies enduring ways to protect your system despite changes in hardware or software technology — be they updates to your system, additions or replacements for your system, or external changes to Internet-based technology that the company connects to.

Coping with Hackers

A *hack* is defined as any unknown or undocumented shortcut that is used on a computer. A hack can substitute for an existing, widely used procedure.

If a hack is merely a shortcut, what is wrong with hacking? Really, nothing is. The important question is, who is doing the hacking and for what purpose? Is the person a clever secretary who has figured out a new way to type documents? Or, is the person a disgruntled employee who wants to retaliate against the CEO personally?

A lot of hair splitting exists regarding the word *hacker*. As understood by computer professionals, however, hackers refer to the "good eggs." Hackers play with software and applications — trying to break them and looking for holes and open back doors. Many hackers work on behalf of their employers and gleefully report their results back to their bosses. The company can then patch, retest, and re-release the software. Some hackers originate outside a company but, instead of maliciously taking advantage of their discoveries, cheerfully document their adventures for the company in the hopes of advancing the software cause.

Crackers, on the other hand, refer to the "bad eggs" who write malicious code, break into networks, and bring about mischief for their own personal — or criminal — benefit. Unfortunately, the media continues to use the term *hacker* for both, confusing the public and failing to distinguish between malicious virus writers and honest employees who are legitimately probing for defects.

Note

As a computer professional, you might also see the terms *white hats* and *black hats*. The white hats refer to the hackers, and the black hats — you guessed it — refer to the crackers.

Rather than using certain definitions or picking colored hats, this book will refer to all computer attackers as *hackers* to make things simple. The overriding issue does not involve singling out certain types of attacks; it does involve looking at your network, examining its weaknesses, and taking the steps that are necessary to protect it. Distinguishing between "good" and "bad" attacks merely wastes precious time that you could use to carry out these actions.

Another time waster is trying to "psych out" a hacker, because psychoanalyzing hacker motives robs time from security tasks. Hackers fall into broad categories, ranging from precocious teenagers to hardened criminals to organized crime. Your computer-security plan needs to be proactive (based on the value and vulnerabilities of your IT assets), not reactive (based on the nebulous psychological profile of an unidentified hacker). If you concentrate on basic security measures, the nature of the attacker is irrelevant.

You might ask, If a determined hacker can get into my system anyway, why should I bother trying to protect it? After all, hacking is not a precise science; it is an art and takes a lot of work. A successful hacker using technical tools might spend hours scanning and probing before finding an open back door. Another hacker might call on the phone, or even visit in person, many times to get that magic password. In spite of all this, wondering whether you should protect your system is like saying, If a thief can get into my home anyway, why should I lock the doors? The answer is, because attackers generally look for the easiest way in. If a thief is walking down your block and trying just to open doors, that thief will move on if your doors have been locked. Similarly, even simple computer-security measures will cause a hacker to proceed to a different system.

No system is impenetrable. But don't make yours easy pickings. Using common sense and following the checklist in this book should give you an adequate measure of security.

Chapter 2

Grouping Attacks into Families

DOZENS OF NETWORK ATTACKS ARE REPORTED daily. Descriptions of them are posted all over the Internet: through news groups, on Web sites, and in hacker chat rooms. It is your job to constantly scour the Web for these descriptions, which can seem like an impossible task. Plus, it gets harder and harder to separate the real accounts from the hoaxes. How do you keep up and keep yourself protected?

The first step is to simplify the confusing array of attacks into groups, or *families* if you will. Each family requires a unique set of responses, and every attack fits into one or more of the following family pairs:

- Common attacks vs. targeted attacks
- Technical attacks vs. human attacks
- Network-level attacks vs. application-level attacks
- Denial attacks vs. misuse

Keep in mind that the most determined hackers are remarkably creative and ingenious, so new families of attacks might appear in the future.

Common Attacks vs. Targeted Attacks

A *common attack* can affect anyone because it is not directed toward any particular individual or organization. Common attacks include the sending of viruses over the Internet, possibly in e-mail attachments that are intended for anyone who will read and download them. Common attacks also include the port scanning of blocks of computers for the purpose of seeing what is open and ripe for picking. (Port scanning is really more reconnaissance than attack, though.)

A *targeted attack* is a premeditated and planned hack against a specific individual or organization. For example, a hacker might try to steal a batch of credit-card numbers from an e-commerce Web site. Or, someone might hire a hacker to steal data from a particular company. Think: Are you in the type of business — banking, for example — that is a potential target, or is your company part of a highly competitive industry? Do you deal with confidential reports or financial information? If so, you could be on someone's hit list.

Technical Attacks vs. Human Attacks

A *technical attack* makes use of hardware, software, or a so-called *hacking software tool*. No human contact is involved. A *human attack,* on the other hand, involves manipulating a person, generally through telephone calls or in-person visits, rather than controlling hardware or software. A human attack is a con game for stealing information, such as a trade secret that can be sold to a competitor. A human attack is also called a *social engineering attack.*

Note that a sophisticated hacker might use a combination of a human attack and a technical attack: first lying to gain access to a facility, for example, and then dropping a keystroke logger onto a computer that sends passwords back to the same hacker.

 **Important**

> Despite the daily mountain of technical attacks that are posted on the Internet, most attacks will be of the human variety. Of those, the majority will come from insiders within your organization.

Network-Level Attacks vs. Application-Level Attacks

A *network-level attack* uses the network itself to break into a system. This type of attack involves using a scanner to find an open port and then exploiting a vulnerability in the application that is running on that port. Examples are the exploitation of Telnet and FTP services. Even the most basic firewall, however, can guard against these attacks by closing a selected port.

Contrastingly, an *application-level attack* uses software to break into a system. This type of attack bypasses network restrictions because the hack is embedded in software or is malware itself. The hack passes undetected through the firewall straight to the end user. Sending a virus as an e-mail attachment is an example of this type of attack. An application-level firewall that is able to examine network traffic for specific types of software can block these attacks.

Denial Attacks vs. Misuse

A *denial attack* prevents your system from being used. This type of attack does little damage per se, but the effect is one of great damage. For example, your company's Web site could appear blank for endless minutes or stop responding altogether. Denial attacks come in two flavors: Denial of Service (DoS) and Distributed Denial of Service (DDoS). The source of a DoS attack is one offending server (either inside or outside the company) that spews out excessive data for the purpose of clogging other servers in the network. A DDoS attack, on the other hand, stems from multiple servers, which can multiply the blockage throughout many networks or even the Internet itself.

Note ———————————————————————————

Data travels through the Internet in a series of related packets. In addition to clogging a network by creating too many packets, a DoS or DDoS attack can also create bad packets that contain instructions to shut down servers in a network. This type of attack is known as a *Smurf attack*.

Misuse refers to three types of hacks: accessing a system without authorization (even if no data is touched); stealing, altering, or destroying data on a system; and taking outright control of a system for a hacker's own purposes. The latter hack often includes using the system as a bridge to reach other systems that exist more deeply in the network.

CHAPTER 3

ASSESSING YOUR SYSTEM

BEFORE YOU CAN SECURE YOUR SYSTEM, YOU need to know what IT assets it contains, the value of each asset, and the potential threats against each asset. (The latter includes the likelihood of each threat and the cost that is associated with that asset's loss or damage.) In other words, you need to *catalog, prioritize,* and *evaluate* the assets in your system — which comprises a classic vulnerability assessment and risk analysis.

To catalog your system, first divide its assets into the following categories:

- Hardware
- Software
- Data
- Processes

Note ────────────────────────────

Some overlap might exist between the Data and Processes categories.

Next, break the categories down further in the following manner:

1. Hardware
    1.1. Servers
        1.1.1. File servers
        1.1.2. E-mail (SMTP) servers
        1.1.3. Authentication servers, such as domain controllers and LDAP servers
        1.1.4. Domain Name System (DNS) servers
        1.1.5. Web and FTP servers
        1.1.6. Proxy servers and dedicated firewalls
        1.1.7. Application servers
    1.2. Workstations and desktops
    1.3. Laptops
    1.4. Mainframes
    1.5. Networking equipment
        1.5.1. Routers
        1.5.2. Gateways
        1.5.3. Switches
        1.5.4. Hubs
        1.5.5. Keyboard, video, mouse (KVM) switches
        1.5.6. Remote access servers
        1.5.7. Wireless access points
        1.5.8. Modems
2. Software
    2.1. In-house software, which consists of applications that were developed by employees for specific company functions
        2.1.1. Local applications (those that are installed on particular users' workstations)
        2.1.2. Distributed applications (those that are installed on servers and accessed remotely)
        2.1.3. Web-based applications
    2.2. Third-party software
        2.2.1. Installed applications that were purchased from outside vendors
        2.2.2. Licensing arrangements for such purchased software

3. Data
    3.1. Intellectual property
    3.2. Documents, including legal papers
    3.3. Databases
        3.3.1. Customer information
        3.3.2. Employee information, including payroll records
        3.3.3. Product catalogs
        3.3.4. Sales and marketing records
        3.3.5. Financial records
    3.4. Strategic plans that are stored on your network
    3.5. Research data and results
4. Processes
    4.1. Documented internal procedures
    4.2. Company policies and management directives
    4.3. Any other data-like items that do not easily fit into the Data category

Now, to prioritize your assets, answer the following questions for each one that you've catalogued:

1. What is the asset's function?
    1.1. Does the asset serve technical departments, nontechnical departments (such as marketing), or both?
2. What does it cost to replace the asset?
    2.1. What is the purchase price of the asset?
    2.2. Would migration to the replacement be difficult (as in the case of a server, for example)?
    2.3. Where does the asset fit into your IT architecture?
        2.3.1. Is the asset physically easy to move and replace?
        2.3.2. Is the asset a vital bottleneck that important data passes through?
3. What is the asset's value to your business?
    3.1. How critical is the asset to the functioning of your business?
    3.2. Would losing the asset cause you to go out of business or just to endure some annoyances?
    3.3. Might losing the asset cause the loss of business to a competitor?

Finally, to evaluate your assets, create a spreadsheet or database that contains the following headings in order from left to right:

- Asset name
- Physical location
- Replacement cost
- Potential threats
- Vulnerability level
- Priority

Enter each of your assets into the spreadsheet or database. Be sure to include the following information, if applicable, for each entry:

1. Asset name
   1.1. A name (such as the IP address, logical name, or other designation) that you have assigned to the asset

2. Physical location
   2.1. The asset's geographic location
      2.1.1. Whether the asset is open to the public or in a secured area that's accessible only to employees
      2.1.2. Whether the asset is in an urban neighborhood, a small town, or a rural area
      2.1.3. Whether the asset is in an area where you fear to walk or a quiet residential neighborhood
      2.1.4. Whether the asset is in a high-rise building or an isolated office
   2.2. The name or number of the room where the asset is located
   2.3. A reference number from a map or diagram that you've already made (by using a program such as Microsoft Visio) for the entire network. The map should contain all the networking devices, labeled with their reference numbers and their relationships to one another.

3. Replacement cost
   3.1. A real monetary value in dollars or whatever the local currency is

4. Potential threats
    4.1. Theft
    4.2. Physical destruction, whether from natural causes or malicious intentions
    4.3. Loss or mutilation of data by hacking
    4.4. Misuse of the system for purposes other than those intended
    4.5. DoS and DDoS attacks
    4.6. Unauthorized access
5. Vulnerability level
    5.1. For each potential threat, a ranking from your own numbered system that represents the likelihood of that threat
6. Priority
    6.1. A ranking from your own numbered system that you enter after all the other columns are filled in

You can now begin to the process of deciding what IT assets to protect; the pecking order of those assets, based on each one's value; and the ways you can protect the assets that you've chosen.

 Note

The Priority column in the spreadsheet or database will help you clarify what to secure first and how much to spend, if anything, on securing each asset.

CHAPTER 4

WRITING YOUR SECURITY POLICY

YOUR SECURITY POLICY PROVIDES THE FOUNDA-
tion and the roadmap for your entire security program — which
consists of all the planning, strategy, and initiatives that are related
to security.

Because it is the most ambiguous part of any security program,
the security policy is the part that is the most prone to failure. No
cookie-cutter template exists for a security policy that is applicable
to all organizations. Because the situations and people involved in
organizations vary, entire books have been written on the subject of
how to create a tailored security policy. This chapter thus presents a
comprehensive guide to the minimum requirements for any security
policy, along with suggestions for making your policy successful.

Note

Two good books that are dedicated to writing tailored security poli-
cies are *Writing Information Security Policies,* Scott Barman (New
Riders, 2001) and *Computer Security Handbook, Fourth Edition,*
Seymour Bosworth and M. E. Kabay, eds. (Wiley, 2002).

Your security policy should be driven by a completed assessment as outlined in Chapter 3, "Assessing Your System." The policy should flow directly from the vulnerability levels and priorities that you set during that assessment. When drafting your security policy, you want to be sure that the content is:

- Easily accessible by all employees and supported by management
- Segmented by department and easily understood by all employees
- Flexible enough to be updated periodically or as the need arises
- Definitive about the acceptable uses of company hardware and software

The first step, which must occur before you begin to write an actual draft, is making sure you can answer the following questions in the affirmative:

1. Does the policy have the buy-in of company executives and upper management?
2. Is a plan in place for communicating the policy throughout the entire organization?
   2.1. Will the policy be located in an accessible place so that employees can refer to it as needed?
3. Will the policy be written in a manner that all employees can understand and thus actually follow?
   3.1. Will the policy take the needs of all departments and internal stakeholders into account?
   3.2. Will the policy be segmented by department, with the content and wording of each segment tailored to that department's needs? (For example, marketing people require different guidelines and wording than, say, data-center staff, who require guidelines that are more technical.)
4. Will the policy exist as a living document that is updated regularly (at least annually)?
   4.1. Will the policy be flexible enough to change as the company's business needs change?

5. Can consistent enforcement be assumed, with clear punishments for violations?

   Let's assume that you are now ready to write the actual security policy. To create a solid, basic policy, you can use the following outline:

1. Statement of purpose
   1.1. From the CEO, company executives, or upper management, the goals for securing the IT enterprise and a pledge of total support for all the steps that the policy contains

2. Organizational structure
   2.1. The reporting structure of the company's IT security personnel
   2.2. For each department in the company, the names of key IT security contacts, including a designated IT security leader

Note

Segmenting your IT security personnel corresponds to segmenting your IT security policy, which should contain a section that is tailored to each department in the company. For example, your network-support staff might need to access a tool that is only available online, so they might need a security contact to occasionally open an FTP port for them. However, if your nontechnical employees don't need to download software from the Internet, that FTP port should always be forbidden to them.

3. Physical security
   3.1. The employees that are allowed into each facility
   3.2. Any rules regarding visitors, outside vendors, and external consultants
   3.3. How physical access to facilities is controlled (for example, with cards or badges)
   3.4. How servers, workstations, and laptops are physically secured from intrusion and theft
   3.5. Whether there is regular monitoring or auditing of people who are entering and exiting facilities

3.6. Whether special standards exist for high-risk IT locations, such as the data center
    3.6.1. If so, what the standards are and how they differ from normal facility-access rules

4. Hiring and termination procedures
    4.1. The guidelines for how to recruit and select new employees
    4.2. Whether new employees will be screened for drug use and criminal records
    4.3. How employees are given security-awareness training when starting employment
    4.4. Each employee's rights and responsibilities regarding IT security
    4.5. The procedures for terminating IT assets and network access

5. Data classification
    5.1. The different classes of data
    5.2. The restrictions on the classes of data, based on the principle of least privilege
    5.3. The standards for encrypting certain confidential data

Note

The *principle of least privilege* states that each user should receive access to only the data that his or her job requires — and only when needed. A user should not receive access at any other time, even if cleared to do so.

6. Access controls
    6.1. The rules for user and administrator accounts
    6.2. The limits on each user who is granted access to the system
    6.3. The way that access is granted to each system
        6.3.1. By user ID and password?
        6.3.2. By an electronic token or magnetic card?
        6.3.3. By a combination of both?
        6.3.4. Differently, depending on the system and department?
    6.4. The limits on the special privileges of administrators
    6.5. The number of administrators that are allowed, who they are, and their purposes
    6.6. The standards for passwords and the rules for their secrecy

7. Operating systems
   7.1. The company standard for the set of allowable operating systems
   7.2. The consequences of using an operating system that is outside the company standard
   7.3. The people who have the authority to install, upgrade, and repair operating systems
   7.4. The frequency that patches should be installed at
       7.4.1. According to a regular schedule, such as weekly or monthly, or as needed?
   7.5. The rules regarding the auditing and logging of operating-system access

 Tip

It is best to keep your systems up-to-date with the latest updates and patches. However, be sure to download them yourself directly from the vendor's Web site. Don't fall for the trick of downloading an attachment from a legitimate-looking e-mail message. Vendors never send updates or patches by e-mail.

8. Hardware and software
   8.1. The standards for third-party client software
       8.1.1. What is allowed on the system
           8.1.1.1. Which word-processing programs, such as Microsoft Word and Sun Microsystems Star-Office Writer?
           8.1.1.2. Which e-mail clients, such as Microsoft Outlook and IBM Lotus Notes?
           8.1.1.3. Which instant-messaging software, if any?
           8.1.1.4. Which Web browsers, such as Microsoft Internet Explorer and Mozilla Firefox?
           8.1.1.5. Which databases, spreadsheets, and reporting tools?
       8.1.2. Whether all employees have the authority for installation on their workstations
           8.1.2.1. If not, who is restricted and who has overall authority?

8.1.3. The standards for patching and upgrading
    8.1.3.1. How often do patches and upgrades occur?
    8.1.3.2. By whom?
    8.1.3.3. Are vendor Web sites regularly monitored for patches and upgrades?
8.2. The standards for allowable hardware, including the authority for installation
    8.2.1. Desktops and workstations
    8.2.2. Laptops
    8.2.3. Servers
    8.2.4. Printers
    8.2.5. Data-storage devices (including Iomega Zip drives, external drives, and USB pen drives)
8.3. The standards for internally developed software
    8.3.1. The guidelines for quality control and installation
    8.3.2. The change-control process for deployment to production
    8.3.3. The people who have the authority to maintain the software postproduction
    8.3.4. The safeguards that exist to check for security holes

 Tip

You should generally disallow instant-messaging software, which can easily spread viruses around a network or be used by malicious attackers to take control of a user's computer.

9. Internet use
9.1. The people who are allowed access to the Internet
9.2. The allowed uses
    9.2.1. Job functions
    9.2.2. Reporting
    9.2.3. Work-related travel
    9.2.4. Other business-related uses
9.3. The prohibited uses
    9.3.1. Gambling (inappropriate for an office and generally illegal)
    9.3.2. Viewing or downloading pornography (can cause security and legal-liability issues)

    9.3.3. Submitting hate mail or other hate-filled content (creates legal-liability and moral issues)

    9.3.4. Personal uses, such as making vacation arrangements or pursuing interests that are not business related

10. E-mail

    10.1. The types of messages that are allowed on the company's e-mail system

        10.1.1. Internal company correspondence

        10.1.2. Memos from management to staff

    10.2. The types of messages that are not allowed

        10.2.1. Jokes, lewd or otherwise

        10.2.2. Virus hoaxes, chain letters, and so on

        10.2.3. Anything personal that is not related to business

        10.2.4. Company data or employee information that is sent externally

    10.3. The rules for monitoring e-mail

        10.3.1. The length of time that messages should be archived for

        10.3.2. Whether any accounts should it be monitored, and if so, when and why?

        10.3.3. Whether all e-mail messages should be logged, and if so, for how long and why?

Tip

Include a warning about e-mail attachments, which continue to be a source of viruses, trojans, and worms. No one should click an attachment — even from someone known personally — unless the attachment was specifically requested.

11. Technical support

    11.1. The information that help-desk staff is allowed to provide

    11.2. How the identity of employees calling the help desk should be verified

    11.3. The clearly delineated roles of the help-desk staff versus the IT security staff

        11.3.1. Who can set up new accounts and passwords, and who can reset them?

12. Virus protection, firewalls, VPNs, and remote access
    12.1. The standards for antivirus software
        12.1.1. The company's preferred (or only allowed) vendor
        12.1.2. How often the software is updated and by whom
            12.1.2.1. Weekly, or as needed (when bulletins are posted)?
    12.2. The standards for firewalls
        12.2.1. The people who have the authority to install, configure, and establish the access rules for firewalls
        12.2.2. Whether firewalls are routinely logged and monitored, and if so, how often
    12.3. The standards for virtual private networks (VPNs)
        12.3.1. The rules for VPN access
        12.3.2. The people who can be granted access
            12.3.2.1. Under what conditions?
        12.3.3. The people who can install the software
    12.4. The standards, if any, for remote access in general
        12.4.1. The standards for modems
        12.4.2. The standards for other remote-access software, such as Symantec pcAnywhere and Citrix GoTo-MyPC Corporate

 Tip

Some good rules of thumb are

- Update antivirus software on all computers at least once a week.
- Follow the instructions when warnings are issued from credible industry sources, such as the CERT Coordination Center.
- Ignore circulating e-mail messages about viruses, even from well-meaning friends. These messages are probably hoaxes.

13. Backups and disaster recovery
    13.1. The data that must be backed up, and how often
    13.2. Where backups are stored and for how long
        13.2.1. On site or at a distant location?

13.3. The preferred backup methods

13.4. The procedures for backing up

13.5. The length of time that backed-up data should be archived for

13.6. The standards for disaster recovery

    13.6.1. The person in charge of administering the disaster-recovery plan

    13.6.2. The general procedures

    13.6.3. How often disaster-recovery and failover exercises are performed

14. Intrusion detection and incident response

14.1. The plan for detecting network intrusions

    14.1.1. The notification procedure for suspected intrusions

        14.1.1.1. The central reporting contact

14.2. The plan for responding to intrusion incidents

    14.2.1. The departments in charge of incident response

        14.2.1.1. The person in charge and the people on the team

    14.2.2. The method of verifying an incident

    14.2.3. The response to an incident

    14.2.4. The procedure for gathering and preserving evidence

15. Additional items

15.1. Anything else from ISO 17799 that applies to your situation

 Note ──────────────────────────────────

ISO 17799 is an internationally recognized standard for benchmarking IT security. For more information, see *http://www.iso-17799.com* (expected to relocate to *http://www.standard-17799.com*) and *http://www.iso17799software.com* (the official ISO 17799 Web site).

CHAPTER 5

TAKING CARE OF PHYSICAL SECURITY

LET'S SAY THAT YOU'VE COMPLETED ASSESSING your IT assets and distributed your security policy. You know what assets to protect, the value of those assets, and how you will protect the assets. However, before you can lower your drawbridge to any invited guests, you need to secure the castle structure itself.

Physically securing the work environment provides the first defense of your IT territory. Yet, too many system administrators leave the door open — literally — while concentrating on the more enticing technical fixes. The problem is that anyone, even the most inept hacker, can break into any computer that is physically accessible.

For example, no password protection exists on Microsoft Windows 98. An attacker would simply click the Cancel button on the logon screen to gain entry! Although this might be an extreme example, think about this: If someone has physical access to a facility and a computer is not bolted down, the easiest way to hack it is to steal it. After the thief has reached a safe location, he or she can play with the computer to gain access by using any number of tools that are freely available on the Internet. The thief can even remove the hard drive and then use the tools to retrieve the data from it.

You might think that password protecting the BIOS would prevent a thief from being able to gain access to the operating system. After all, the thief could not boot from any drive without knowledge of that password. Well, forget about it. An attacker can bypass any BIOS security and boot up the operating system simply by using a screwdriver.

So, how do you physically protect your computer systems? To begin to do so, go through the following checklist:

1. Data-center location
   1.1. If the data center is located in a densely populated urban area, make sure that the building is unmarked and not easily noticed.
      1.1.1. Otherwise, surround the building with a fence that is 8 feet high and topped with barbed wire.
   1.2. If possible, locate the data center in its own, freestanding building. This way, the data center is isolated from people that might casually walk in.
      1.2.1. If a separate building is not possible, locate the data center on a floor other than the first so that it is not easily accessible.
         1.2.1.1. If you locate the data center in the basement, provide for adequate flood protection.
   1.3. Construct the building or portion of the building that contains the data center to either be windowless or have frosted and barred windows.

2. Computer rooms
   2.1. Lock all doors to these rooms.
   2.2. Tuck all network cabling, punch boards, and junction boxes out of sight.
      2.2.1. Either behind walls, under floors, or above drop ceilings
   2.3. Secure the assets in these rooms in accordance with their rankings from your risk assessment.
      2.3.1. Secure more-valuable assets more securely.
   2.4. Provide only a single access point, such as one door, so that the entrance can be controlled.

How to Break into a Computer that Is Right at Your Fingertips

The essential tools for the physical hacker are the following:

- Phillips screwdriver
- KNOPPIX CD
- KNOPPIX boot floppy disk
- USB key (at least 256 MB)

To bypass a BIOS password, an attacker can use any of the following methods (screwdriver required):

- Removing the hard drive from the computer and placing it in another computer that has an accessible BIOS
- Moving the appropriate jumper on the motherboard to reset the BIOS settings to the factory defaults (if the jumper exists on that particular motherboard)
- Removing the CMOS battery from the motherboard and then putting it back in, which resets the BIOS settings to the factory defaults

If the BIOS is not password protected, the attacker doesn't even need a screwdriver. He or she can hack into a Windows- or Linux-based computer by using only two items: a KNOPPIX CD and a USB key. KNOPPIX is a Linux distribution that is available for free at *http://www. knoppix.com* and that can be burned onto a single CD. The attacker can boot KNOPPIX from the CD and then copy everything from the hard drive to the USB key. (If the BIOS has been set to disallow booting from the CD drive, the attacker needs only one additional item: a KNOPPIX boot floppy disk, which is available from the same site as the KNOPPIX CD.)

When finished, all the attacker needs to do is remove the KNOPPIX CD, the USB key, and the KNOPPIX boot floppy disk (if used) and then restart the computer. Windows or Linux will start, and no evidence that anyone ever tampered with the system will exist.

2.4.1. Employ one or more access-control methods, making sure that the level of control is commensurate with the assessment rankings.
- 2.4.1.1. Pass cards with magnetic stripes and their readers
- 2.4.1.2. Electronic locks that require PIN numbers
- 2.4.1.3. Double doors, mantraps, or turnstiles
  - 2.4.1.3.1. To prevent piggybacking, have someone guard or watch the entrance
- 2.4.1.4. Surveillance cameras
- 2.4.1.5. Biometric systems
- 2.4.1.6. Human security guards, and possibly watchdogs

2.5. If you have drop ceilings, make sure that the walls extend above them to the actual room ceilings.
- 2.5.1. Drop ceilings with low walls can easily be scaled from neighboring offices.

2.6. Provide adequate protection against electrical fires, which are likely to affect computer equipment.

3. Individual workstations
3.1. To prevent physical theft, use cables to attach all workstations to the walls or the floor.
3.2. Make sure that workstations are free of sticky notes — or any notes, for that matter — that have passwords written on them.
3.3. Place workstations so that the monitors are not visible from exterior windows.
- 3.3.1. A well-placed telescope in a neighboring office can allow a hacker to sift passwords or other data from the screen of an employee at work. It happens.

3.4. Encourage users to lock their workstations whenever they walk away, be it for the day or even a quick break. To do so, users can click the Lock The Desktop icon on the Linux taskbar, for example.

3.5. Set a BIOS password.
- 3.5.1. Even though a BIOS password can be breached, it could be the one thing that causes an attacker to move on.

Important

Passwords should never be written down — under any circumstances. Doing so is the equivalent of leaving the key under the doormat.

4. People flow
    4.1. Make sure that each authorized employee has a company-issued picture ID badge.
        4.1.1. Make sure that employees are required to wear these badges at all times when on company property.
        4.1.2. Color-code the badges based on department or job function so that it's clear who is authorized to access different areas.
    4.2. Issue strict guidelines to vendors and consultants who are on long-term assignments regarding what they can access, and provide them with badges that identify them as having limited privileges.
    4.3. Verify that each visitor has an appointment with an employee, provide each such visitor with a temporary badge that indicates "visitor" status, and escort visitors at all times when they are on company premises.
    4.4. Check with vendors regarding unannounced changes in delivery schedules or personnel.
        4.4.1. Why is a different UPS driver coming at such an odd hour today?
        4.4.2. Who is that new person on the night cleaning crew, and why is he or she snooping around a workstation instead of dusting the desk?
5. Data destruction
    5.1. Locate paper shredders so that they are accessible to employees at all levels.
    5.2. Purchase shredders that confetti-cut documents or that cut along crossed diagonal lines.
        5.2.1. Technology is available for reassembling documents that were shredded into long, thin, straight strips by traditional shredders.

5.3. Destroy all CDs (which are optical media) by physically destroying them (shredding, scratching, or cutting into pieces).

5.4. Destroy all magnetic media by degaussing, demagnetizing, zeroing out, or physically destroying them.

    5.4.1. Floppy disks

    5.4.2. Hard drives

    5.4.3. Tape reels

    5.4.4. Zip disks

    5.4.5. USB cards

Important

If you simply format a piece of magnetic media and then toss it in the garbage, a hacker can use tools that are freely available on the Internet to retrieve data, password files, and more. These are the same tools that computer-forensics experts use to scan employees' disk drives for unauthorized files: pornography, confidential company memos, and so on.

6. Garbage

6.1. Practice safe disposal, which means destroying all data before tossing in the garbage.

6.2. Place your garbage bins in locked and secured areas.

6.3. Allow only authorized employees and chosen vendors to have access to your garbage area.

Note

The fine art of dumpster diving is a hacker classic. The garbage can contain endless riches — such as discarded passwords, lists of employee names with company IDs, and other seemingly unimportant information that a clever social engineer can weave into a tale to gain access to your system.

CHAPTER 6

MANAGING HUMAN RESOURCES

NOW THAT YOU HAVE PHYSICALLY SECURED your territory, it's time to allow people — invited guests, of course — to come in. However, it's a worn-out cliché that people make up the weakest link in any security program. That is, people are unpredictable and more likely to be manipulated than any hardened machine. So, no matter how strong your technical defenses are, an inside employee who reveals unauthorized information defeats every security control that you have worked so hard to establish.

Considering that most attacks against your network will come from people trying to con their way in — that is, from social engineers — and that of those, most will come from insiders within your organization, careful hiring is equally as important as locking down your systems by technical means.

Unlike the technical guidelines in this book for which the settings are clearly black or white, the guidelines in this chapter provide more of a best approach than a precise tool. They offer a good measure of protection but are far from foolproof.

Tip

It isn't always easy to tell who is likely to be manipulated or by what and when. Whenever possible, a technical security control — which can be precisely monitored and tweaked — is more favorable than a fickle human control.

The general spheres of human-resource management that relate to security are the following:

1. Hiring policies
2. Termination procedures
3. Strategies for defeating social engineers

Hiring Policies

Managing human resources begins even before a new employee walks through the door for the first time. For security reasons, follow the pre-employment and employment procedures that are listed here:

1. Prior to employment
    1.1. Thoroughly review the resume and employment application.
        1.1.1. Verify all employment for the past five years.
        1.1.2. Look for any unusual or unexplained gaps.
        1.1.3. Verify details — including dates.
            1.1.3.1. University and graduate-school education.
            1.1.3.2. Military service and discharge details.
            1.1.3.3. Licenses, certifications, professional designations, and professional memberships.
            1.1.3.4. Special skills. (Does he or she really speak French as claimed on the resume?)
    1.2. Verify and call all references.
        1.2.1. People generally supply references who will provide glowing recommendations, so don't rely on them as the sole criteria for employment.

1.3. Screen the potential employee.
    1.3.1. Drug tests
    1.3.2. Criminal-background check
    1.3.3. Credit report (useful mostly for verifying employment)

Tip

Some fraud convictions carry sentences of under two years. Such a short gap can easily be papered over on a resume and go unnoticed. Be sure that the applicant really worked where claimed and wasn't an involuntary guest in a state or federal penitentiary.

Tip

The eternal question: Should you hire that so-called reformed hacker? He seemed so charming and sincere in the interview; she did so cleverly figure out how to gain access to your computer network. And they sure seem to know an awful lot about you and your operation. However, the short answer is no. Although there are those who have, or can be, reformed, no shortage exists of good hacking types (in other words, skilled IT security professionals) who have always stayed on the right side of the law. Still, the choice is up to you. Just be aware of the risk if you choose to hire that ex-felon.

2. During employment
    2.1. Review the company's IT security policy with all employees and be sure that they understand it.
    2.2. Make adherence to security policies a part of the regular or annual performance review.
    2.3. Reward employees for following security procedures.
    2.4. Conduct regular training programs to increase security awareness.
        2.4.1. Include role playing or other methods that teach employees how to spot potential social engineers and hacking attempts.

2.5. Provide a single point of contact — either one individual or a team that rotates on-call responsibilities among its members — where employees can confidentially report security breaches.

2.6. To minimize panic and the inadvertent spreading of hoaxes, advise employees not to spread rumors about viruses or other attacks that were not received from authoritative sources.

2.7. Supply employees with regular bulletins about attacks that they should be on the lookout for.

2.8. Be sensitive to company changes that might cause a disgruntled employee to release internal information. Deal with these situations immediately and don't let them fester.

2.8.1. Changes in job roles or titles

2.8.2. Pay cuts or freezes

2.8.3. Pending layoffs

2.8.4. Mergers and acquisitions

2.8.5. Sudden or frequent reorganizations

2.8.6. Unfavorable media attention toward the company

Termination Procedures

You do the best to hire the best, but even then, employees sometimes need to be terminated. Regardless of whether the reason is performance-based or due to business losses, you should employ the following safeguards to protect your IT environment:

1. Review all your termination procedures with the legal and human-resources departments, and obtain their approval.

2. Take the following steps prior to terminating an employee:

2.1. Inventory all systems, networks, applications, and data that the employee has access to.

2.2. Check whether any unauthorized or rogue hardware or software exists on the employee's systems.

2.3. List all the employee's user and administrative accounts.

2.3.1. Particularly note any administrative accounts that include special privileges.

2.4. Check whether any orphaned accounts exist, and if so, trace their ownership. If they are no longer being used, shut them down.

2.5. Coordinate the termination date and time with the IT-security, building-security, and human-resources departments. If possible, plan for a time when the system will not be busy, so the IT staff can disable the employee's accounts without distractions.

3. Quickly take the following steps at the moment of termination (before the employee is out the door, if possible):

   3.1. Remove all physical access devices (badges, ID cards, access tokens, keys, and card keys) from the employee's possession.

   3.2. Remove any network-access software, such as VPN clients and RAS software, from the employee's possession.

   3.3. Lock out access to the employee's workstation.

   3.4. Cancel and remove all system and network accounts.

   3.5. Escort the employee from the premises.

4. After termination, be sure that the IT staff checks the logs of the previously inventoried systems for any entry attempts by the terminated employee.

   4.1. Add rules to any Intrusion Detection Systems for checking the same.

5. If the person was employed either by the IT department or as a software developer with access to restricted systems, create backups of network configurations and crucial applications or data. In case of sabotage, you will then be able to quickly rebuild the damaged network or system.

Strategies for Defeating Social Engineers

Sure, you want to do an outstanding job and it is part of your job to be helpful, but resist the temptation to provide more information than requested, especially to a stranger. Comply only with the matter at hand, and stick to the part that is related to your specific job function. Remembering that the three key principles for defeating social engineers are verify, verify, and verify, be sure that all employees abide by the following guidelines:

1. If you receive an unsolicited or unexpected telephone call, check up on the caller.
    1.1. If you have caller ID, check whether the call is internal or external.
    1.2. If the call is internal, perform the following procedures:
        1.2.1. Verify the caller's identity.
        1.2.2. Check whether the caller is listed in the company directory.
        1.2.3. Phone the caller's supervisor to verify the caller's request.
        1.2.4. Keep in mind that an internal call is not necessarily safe. An off-site attacker can manipulate the phone system to appear as if he or she is calling from the premises. Or, an attacker could be on the premises, having used a prior ruse to gain entry.
    1.3. If the call is external, perform the following procedures:
        1.3.1. Get the caller's full name, company name, and return phone number.
        1.3.2. Verify that the return phone number matches the caller-ID display.
        1.3.3. Verify that the caller will allow you to call back later at the given number.
            1.3.3.1. The caller might simply hang up here, and you have just foiled a potential scammer!
        1.3.4. Phone the company that the caller claims to represent and verify that he or she does, in fact, represent that company.

 Tip

Always verify the identity of any caller — even if that person claims to be the CEO or another high-level executive in the company. If the company takes security seriously, you will be rewarded for your alertness and not considered obstinate. Legitimate requests by upper management — even during a business emergency — are always handled through proper channels.

Tip

Skilled social engineers have done their homework and can sound just like insiders. They might say that they work in a distant department or in the technical-support department — and are just trying to help you out. They know company lingo and just enough of the inside scoops to sound legitimate. They may even claim another employee, including the employee's ID number, as a reference.

2. When a visitor arrives at the front desk or receptionist area, perform the following procedures:

    2.1. Verify the visitor's identity by asking to see an official picture ID — even if the visitor is wearing a uniform, particularly that of a delivery company.

    2.2. If the visitor has an appointment, call the employee to verify it.

 Tip

Anyone can buy a uniform and fake ID that resemble those of even the most common delivery companies: UPS, FedEx, and so on. Be especially alert to unusual behavior or an unfamiliar driver — particularly at odd hours — or to a driver that tries to sneak in during a commotion. In these situations, verify by calling the delivery company, if possible.

3. Keep the following tip-offs to attempted social engineering in mind:

    3.1. Asking for confidential information as part of a story

    3.2. Claiming to be from the technical-support department and requesting a password

    3.3. Pulling rank, and threatening action against you for not complying with a request

    3.4. Being in a hurry, and rushing you to provide something according to a deadline

3.5. Excessively chattering to try and loosen you up, or using long and complicated stories with convoluted excuses

Important ──────────────────────────────

Never give your password to anyone for any reason. This can't be emphasized enough. A system administrator, or anyone working at your company's help desk, for that matter, can access your system without your password and shouldn't need it for any reason. If you forget it or run into another problem with it, these same staff members can reset your password so that you can start from scratch.

4. Avoid succumbing to the following offers and requests:
   4.1. Free offers
   4.2. Free magazine subscriptions, or subscription offers that are cloaked in survey requests
   4.3. Surveys, marketing or otherwise
   4.4. Sales calls
   4.5. Sweepstakes awards, because legitimate winners are notified by registered mail
   4.6. School projects
   4.7. Requests for the name or ID of any employee, including yourself
   4.8. Requests for the company directory or where such information is available
   4.9. Requests for any company information other than the main telephone number

As nasty as some of the previous guidelines might seem, they can be real lifesavers. For example, social engineers sometimes call several people in an organization and obtain a snippet of information each time. They use the snippets to build a convincing identity that later allows them to fool their way into the company. However, if any link in the chain is broken, their gig is up. Social engineers are like cockroaches that work in the dark until someone turns on the light, and then they scatter. Be the one who turns on the light.

CHAPTER 7

PUTTING SOFTWARE ACCESS CONTROLS IN PLACE

IT IS NOW TIME FOR YOU TO DECIDE WHO CAN access what as well as how they can get to it. In other words, you need to create *software access controls* for all of your data. To do so, you need to segregate your people into groups that compose a hierarchy based on people's ranks, their need to know, and the sensitivity of the data.

Note

It is important to distinguish between the two types of access controls: hardware and software. Chapter 5, "Taking Care of Physical Security," discussed hardware access controls (sometimes called just *hardware controls*). This chapter discusses software access controls (or *software controls*), which restrict access to systems, applications, and data after a user has physically accessed a computer.

Putting software access controls in place consists of the following three-step process:

1. Creating a classification system for all of your data
2. Creating a hierarchy of groups that can access the data

3. Choosing the software authentication methods you will use to protect the data

When implementing this process, keep in mind the following categories of people who are involved in handling data:

- Data owners
- Data custodians
- Data users

Based on the security policy, *data owners* define both the levels in the classification system and the groups that make up the hierarchy. *Data custodians* manage the data on behalf of the owners by setting up and managing the classification system and the groups. *Data users* are those who need to actually access the data to fulfill their job functions.

Classifying Your Data

Clearly, the data-classification needs of military and government organizations are different from those of retail businesses and software-development companies, for example. But every organization, no matter its stripe, needs a system that consists of basic classification levels, which are presented in order from the least to the most sensitive in Table 7.1.

The classification system that Table 7.1 describes is overly general; you must modify it to meet your particular organization's needs. When doing so, abide by the following rules:

- Be sure that upper management supports your data-classification system.
- Create a clear separation between data owners and data custodians.
- Develop well-defined and clear-cut criteria for describing the classification levels.
- Periodically review the levels and modify them as needed.
- Implement a logging system that records when data at sensitive levels was accessed and by whom.

Table 7.1

A basic data-classification system

Classification level	Description
Public/Unrestricted	Information at this level is freely available in the media, on the Web, or in print. The key fact is that revealing this information will not cause any harm to the organization.
Restricted	Restricted data is best revealed discreetly but otherwise won't cause harm to the organization. Examples are financial information and profit forecasts.
Confidential	Confidential data, which might cause harm if released, is restricted to use within the organization. Examples include trade secrets, competitive information, and programming code.
Secret/Private	Releasing information at this level might cause serious harm to the organization. Examples are troop movements for the military and employee medical information for a business.
Top secret	Disclosing top-secret data would cause grave damage to an organization, threatening its existence. For the government, an example is espionage information. For a business, an example is the set of blueprints for an as-yet-undisclosed product offering.

Creating a Hierarchy of Groups

After you have classified all of your data, you need to segregate your users into a hierarchy of groups. Be sure that the hierarchy breaks along the following functional fault lines:

- Functional area or department

    Place the marketing and accounting departments, for example, into their own groups. Further divide these main groups, as needed, into subgroups for individual projects within the respective departments. Furthermore, consider peoples' ranks and job titles. Keeping in mind that the groups compose a hierarchy, create groups within departments or within subgroups that have more privileges than others, if necessary. For example, you might need a group whose members must be at or above the vice-presidential level. At the same time, one of those vice presidents could be a member of another, less restricted group.

- Special projects

  Set up temporary groups for special projects and dismantle them as each project is completed. Usually, the group members already belong to other groups and will continue to do so before, during, and after the special project.

- IT managers and staff

  Based on functionality and rank, create separate groups for the different IT departments just as you would for all the other departments. For example, a group that consists of the networking staff would have access to the network servers on which they perform routine maintenance, whereas a separate group of database managers would have access to the database servers. Additionally, all your IT people will generally need access to other groups so they can set up the user accounts and group assignments that are handed to them from other parts of the company.

When creating and managing the groups, abide by the following rules:

- Each group should be matched to a data-classification level and then further subdivided on a need-to-know basis.

  Suppose that Sally in marketing as well as her boss are members of one group for a particular project. The boss is additionally a member of another, higher-level group that has access to future marketing projects of a competitive nature. The members of Sally's group are then added to and deleted from the higher-level group on a need-to-know basis.

- Groups can overlap.

  A user can belong to an unlimited number of groups and, depending on the operating system, a whole group can be a member of another group.

- Groups can always change.

  At any time, you can add or delete a member from a group, create an entirely new group, or remove a group altogether.

- You should remove orphaned and unneeded groups.

  You should conduct regular audits of system accounts to check for group activity. Immediately remove any inactive groups — which contain accounts that could be a hacker's hidden playground.

Choosing Software Authentication Methods

For each asset, the software authentication method (or methods) that you choose should flow from the priority and vulnerability levels that you set when evaluating your assets in Chapter 3, "Assessing Your System." The possible methods, which are listed in order from the most secure to the least, are the following:

1. Biometric solutions (used in conjunction with hardware access controls)
   1.1. Iris or retina scanning (almost impossible to fool)
   1.2. Voice or face recognition
   1.3. Fingerprint scanning (can be mimicked with difficulty)
2. Card systems and token devices
   2.1. Smart cards that contain embedded chips, such as the RSA SecurID 5100 smart card
   2.2. Card keys with magnetic stripes that are swiped through a reader
   2.3. RSA SecurID 6100 tokens, which each generate a one-time password
3. Password systems
   3.1. Kerberos
   3.2. Windows NT Challenge/Response
   3.3. Cryptographic Handshake Authentication Protocol (CHAP) or Password Authentication Protocol (PAP)

Note ───────────────────────────────────

Using two methods together is called a *two-factor authentication system*. To allow logging on to a server, for example, you could use a password system such as Windows NT Challenge/Response and require the temporary password that is generated by an RSA SecurID 6100 USB token — and this combination would be stronger than either method alone would be.

Password Practices

Because password systems comprise the most common authentication methods, a few words are in order about safe password practices. To begin with, you need to know that hackers generally crack passwords in one of two ways: by a brute force attack or by a dictionary attack. When instituting a *brute force attack*, a hacker repeatedly guesses at passwords but does not use any password-cracking programs. When instituting a *dictionary attack*, the hacker runs a program that compares a "dictionary" of words and names with a password file. Often, the dictionary contains a long list of commonly chosen username and password combinations.

Note ───────────────────────────────────

Two commonly used password-cracking programs are John the Ripper and @stake LC (previously named L0phtCrack). The former is freely available, whereas the latter is a commercial product that system administrators use to recover lost passwords and that hackers, like anyone else, can purchase. Additional programs exist that are just a few clicks away — through any hacker Web site or by searching with Google.

For password creation, consider the following suggestions:

• Increase the password length.

Each additional character exponentially increases the number of combinations that a brute force attack or a dictionary attack needs to try. The longer an attempted attack takes,

Some Good and Bad Passwords

An example of a strong password is **2xJfg!29bh** because of the following:

- The 10-character length
- The lack of dictionary words
- The extreme unlikelihood of being guessed by a brute force attacker

An example of a lousy password is **suzy25** because of the following:

- The likelihood of being guessed by a brute force attacker, given that *Suzy* is probably the name of the user, the user's wife, or the user's daughter.
- The likelihood of being guessed by a brute force attacker or matched by a dictionary program, given that 25 might be the user's age or an increment of the previous password. (Say that the password was **suzy24** before the last required password update. Big deal.)
- The short length, which makes cracking it a cakewalk for a dictionary attacker. Password-cracking dictionaries are full of such short words and names.

So, how about **$uzy25**? you might think. Well, no dice. Most dictionary programs include such simple substitutions and will still match the correct password.

the likelier it is that the hacker will move on to more fertile territory.

- Don't use any words, names, or combinations thereof that can be found in any dictionary.

  Instead, use a combination of uppercase letters, lowercase letters, numbers, and other characters. The more complicated, obscure, and incomprehensible the password is, the greater the defense is against a dictionary attack.

- Never use personal information.

  Steer clear of the names of spouses, children, other family members, pets, and friends; United States social security numbers or your country's national ID number; birthdays or parts of birthdays, such as the year of your birth; and your address or any combination of your street name and address number. These items provide easy ammunition for a brute force attack because they're generally available through social engineering or identity theft.

To carry out the best procedures regarding password safety, put the following into practice:

- Lock out an account after three failed logon attempts.

    At this point, require the user to call the IT security department to reset the password. This practice offers the easiest defense against a brute force attack. Three strikes and you're out — no exceptions.

- Change passwords according to a regular schedule.

    The system should prompt and force each user to change his or her password monthly, at a minimum, or every 90 days, at most. This practice offers a strong defense against both brute force attacks and dictionary attacks. If a person or a cracking program takes longer than the password's lifetime to figure out that password, a hacker has no chance of accessing the account.

- When you reset a password, make it a one-time password that is good for a limited duration.

    As the system administrator or IT security contact in charge of issuing passwords, supply a one-time password to the user that is good for, say, 24 hours. When the user logs on that one time, he or she should be prompted to enter a new password.

- Make sure that dead passwords never come back to life.

    After a password has expired or been locked out, the system should prevent the user from ever using that password on that system again. Not all operating systems can boast this feature; use only one that can. Hackers sometimes wait for passwords that they've previously cracked to be reincarnated.

- Require a different password for each account that belongs to the same user.

  If a user has the same password on every system that he or she can access, all a hacker needs is that one password to get into all of the accounts: e-mail, Web, database, and so on.

- Make sure that logon screens offer no hints after a failed logon attempt.

  If the logon fails, the user ID and password fields should be cleared, and a message such as **User ID or password incorrect** should appear. To avoid providing a potential hacker the hint that one half of the puzzle has been solved, the message should not specify which one was incorrect.

- Encrypt password files on desktops or authentication servers.

  On a Windows-based system, encrypt the SAM file. On a Unix-based system, encrypt the /etc/passwd file. A common hacker trick is to gain access to these files, which contain lists of hashed user IDs and passwords, and to then try and crack the hash coding by using John the Ripper. By encrypting the file itself, you place the user IDs and passwords out of reach.

- To prevent replay attacks, require users to log out of Web sites and applications.

  If a user remains logged on to a Web site or application after all activity is complete, a remote attacker could grab the URL (which contains logon information), paste the URL into a browser at some future time, and replay the session.

- Avoid password managers that store user IDs and passwords for convenience.

  Windows and Linux both provide this capability. On the surface, it's a great time saver, because after you log on to an application or Web site for the first time, the manager automatically fills in any logon screen and requires only that you click to confirm. However, these managers store the logon information in files that hackers can grab and later open to lift user IDs and passwords.

Chapter 8

Securing E-mail

BY AND LARGE, THE REMAINDER OF THIS BOOK
deals with technical solutions to security issues rather than the conceptual, policy, and personnel matters that have been discussed so far. Because e-mail is the most widely used Internet application, it will be addressed first.

As one of the least secure Internet applications, e-mail is also one of the most hackable. In the world of e-mail hacking, two basic approaches exist: sniffing and spoofing. *Sniffing* consists of intercepting and reading an e-mail message while it's on the network wire. This hack creates a problem for both the sender and the recipient, but only the sender has the power to protect the message — through encryption, for example.

Spoofing consists of masking the sender's true identity (e-mail address). The hacker either crafts a bogus address or uses the address of another, legitimate sender. Clearly, this hack creates a problem for the message recipient, who can easily be duped by the bogus message.

E-mail presents two sets of security issues: one for sending messages and another for receiving them. Here is the security checklist for sending messages:

1. Determine whether to encrypt message contents and, if so, what encryption technique to use.

1.1. Make these decisions on a per-department basis. Look at the level of security that is dictated by your security policy for each department and its assets.

1.2. Note that encryption is a complex topic of its own that is beyond the scope of this book. Suffice it to say that most e-mail encryption techniques fall into one of the following categories:

    1.2.1. Pretty Good Privacy (PGP)

        1.2.1.1. Exists as a separate application from the e-mail client

        1.2.1.2. Uses public key encryption

        1.2.1.3. Remains free and downloadable from the Internet

    1.2.2. Secure/Multipurpose Internet Mail Extensions (S/MIME)

        1.2.2.1. Exists as part of the e-mail client installation

        1.2.2.2. Uses public key encryption (therefore, similar to PGP)

        1.2.2.3. Allows secure messages to be sent between e-mail clients that both understand S/MIME

2. Be sure that technical employees use multiple e-mail accounts and aliases to protect the privacy of the company.

2.1. Allow such employees to use personal accounts when seeking work-related information from newsgroups — even though such permission contravenes the security policy for nontechnical employees.

2.2. Take care that the account names and aliases are hard to guess (and do not contain the individuals' names nor the company name).

 Important

Because messages that are posted to newsgroups are accessible to the online world forever, allowing technical employees to use personal accounts and aliases is a must. Consider the fact that a favored hacker procedure is using Google to search for *@yourcompany.com* during the reconnaissance phase of a planned attack. It is better, therefore, for all your postings to originate from an apparently unknown source.

Generally, you need to send e-mail messages to receive them back. The exceptions are unsolicited messages that are legitimate (such as advertisements that you agree to receive when you register on a company's Web site) and spam. Keeping these facts in mind, all employees should be aware of the following security checklist for receiving e-mail messages:

1. Be on the lookout for unscrupulous messages.
   1.1. Spam messages, which are often scams
   1.2. Infections (viruses, trojans, and worms)
2. Scan for the following to check for spam:
   2.1. In the **From:** line:
       2.1.1. A sender that you don't know (although knowing the sender is not always foolproof, as described later in this chapter)
   2.2. In the **Subject:** line:
       2.2.1. Pornography or adult solicitation
       2.2.2. Sales of Pfizer VIAGRA or other prescription medications

---

How to Send Fake E-mail Messages (Better Known as Spoofing)

To send a spoofed message, a hacker must perform the following steps:

1. Obtain a password through sniffing, hacking, or social engineering.
2. Gain access to the e-mail (SMTP) server by using Telnet or Netcat to access port 25 (the SMTP port).
   The e-mail application will now be available from the command line.
3. When requested by the e-mail application, enter a message with a bogus address or the address of another, legitimate sender.
4. Send the message.

Note that all e-mail applications require a sender's e-mail address to work. However, they don't require the sender to be legitimate or to have an account on the sending server.

2.2.3. Products that enlarge sexual organs or other body parts

2.2.4. Quotes for real estate, mortgages, refinancing, loans, or insurance

2.2.5. Get-rich-quick schemes

2.2.6. Private-detective services or monitoring products

2.2.7. Home-improvement products

2.2.8. Offers for home employment

2.2.9. Offers for antivirus software

2.2.10. Urban legends, jokes, or conspiracy theories

2.2.11. Gibberish combinations of letters, misspellings, or unusual spellings such as *V.I.A.G.R.A* (which are attempts at bypassing spam filters)

2.3. In the header (which is displayed in the body of the message):

2.3.1. A sender e-mail address that does not match the one in the **From:** line

2.3.2. An unknown or untraceable source IP address or Web address

 Note _____

Some e-mail services and clients hide the header to avoid cluttering the beginning of a message with undecipherable gobbledygook. In those cases, you can still request that the header be displayed. For information about how to do so, see your e-mail application's Help documentation.

3. Do not open, reply to, or keep suspected spam messages.

3.1. Do not open a suspected spam message — even if no attachment exists. In the past, you could safely open a message provided that you didn't click an attachment. However, today's e-mail messages can be sent in HTML format, and HTML code can contain viruses.

3.2. Do not reply to spam under any circumstances. If you happen to open a message by mistake, never click the link at the bottom that allows you to be "removed from future mailings." Any reply perversely tells the spammer that you're a "live one" and that your e-mail address should be kept active for future spammings.

3.3. Delete spam messages on the spot. They waste your time and fill the limited space that is allotted to your e-mail account.

4. Do not accept free offers, join mailing lists, or make online purchases.

4.1. You can't stop living, but you can distribute your e-mail address as moderately as possible. Every time you give your e-mail address to a new person, you run the risk that the person will give — or sell — it to someone else, resulting in spam from somewhere along the chain.

5. Be aware of phishing, which is in vogue with hackers these days.

5.1. When a hacker goes *phishing*, he or she sets up a bogus Web site that looks like it belongs to a legitimate business. However, the site claims that the company needs additional information, or it presents some other ruse. A request is made for the user's name, address, social security number, bank account number, or other private information. Users get to these sites by clicking links in spam messages that they receive.

6. Be aware of the following tip-offs to potential infections:

6.1. A sender that you don't know.

6.1.1. However, knowing the sender is not always foolproof. Some viruses send themselves to everyone in a victim's address book and even generate authentic-looking subject lines.

6.2. An unusual subject line from a sender that you do know.

6.2.1. Why is your boss sending you a message with *I Love You* in the subject line? (If you remember it, that was an actual virus.) Your company has an airtight sexual-harassment policy, and your boss doesn't really love you anyway.

Phishing: The New Fake E-mail and How to Spot It

A recent e-mail message, cleverly spoofed from Microsoft Corporation, claimed to contain a patch for a known security flaw. The "patch" turned out to be a tool that allowed the hacker to access the recipient's computer and steal account information. Microsoft does allow users to subscribe by e-mail to a newsletter that contains security alerts. However, the e-mail message never contains patches or any other attachments. Instead, it provides a link to a Microsoft site which, in turn, supplies details about the issue and a link to the official, downloadable patch.

Keep in mind that companies never use e-mail to ask for your password, social security number, or bank account information. Spoofed e-mail messages look official and can resemble a legitimate warning that your account is about to expire. However, banks and other companies don't send repeated messages to "verify" your account. These dangerous impersonation scams can result in monetary theft at the least and identity theft at the worst, so check the following in all such messages:

- Is the URL that the message directs you to exactly the same as the URL in the sender's e-mail address? It's a cakewalk for a hacker to steal the logo and graphics from a company's Web site and then plant them on a bogus site that uses a similar — but not identical — URL.

- Does the message, although official-looking, contain misspellings or grammatical errors? Many of these scams are perpetrated by hackers outside the United States who have less-than-perfect English-language skills.

If you get a suspicious message, all it takes for verification is one phone call to the alleged sender. Your call will also alert the company if it isn't already aware of the scam.

    6.3. An attachment.

        6.3.1. Attachments are by far the largest source of virus infections. Even attachments from well-meaning friends could contain viruses, trojans, or worms, so never open an attachment that you did not request. Furthermore, discourage others from sending you attachments. Resumes, for example, should be submitted through the company's Web site.

        6.3.2. If you are expecting an attachment, use antivirus software to scan it either before downloading (allowed by some clients) or after downloading to an isolated location.

7. If you sign up for a newsletter, choose to receive it in ASCII (not HTML) format.

    7.1. An HTML file can hide malicious code, which your browser can pass on to your system. An ASCII file can't hide malicious code because it contains plain text only.

8. Ignore messages that contain warnings about viruses or other security matters, except for those from the CERT Coordination Center or one of the major antivirus vendors.

    8.1. These messages are usually hoaxes that are meant to create unnecessary panic. Do not forward these messages, even if they come from well-meaning friends. Like spam, they clog e-mail servers and fill up hard drives.

    As an IT professional, you should also implement the following security measures regarding your SMTP server:

1. Maintain a dedicated SMTP server for e-mail and put it behind a firewall.

    1.1. A dedicated server can be temporarily shut down during an attack without disrupting your other network servers. Access should be severely restricted to system administrators who are in charge of e-mail.

2. Be sure that your SMTP server is not inadvertently being used to relay spam.

    2.1. Be sure that the server only sends and receives SMTP traffic but does not forward any of it.

3. Install a spam filter at your gateway.

   3.1. This evolving technology is still hit-or-miss, but it can sometimes fit the bill for your particular needs. Such software needs to be tested to be sure it doesn't admit some types of spam or block any legitimate messages.

4. Configure the server so that it checks for attachments and removes those with executable-file extensions, such as *.exe*, *.vbs*, and *.scr*.

5. Install antivirus software (with the latest signatures) on your SMTP server and on all computers that are running e-mail clients.

CHAPTER 9

PROTECTING YOUR SYSTEM AGAINST VIRUSES, TROJANS, AND WORMS

VIRUSES, TROJANS, AND WORMS ARE KNOWN collectively as *malware* and have the following characteristics in common:

- Consist of malicious programming code that is installed on a user's system — without that user's knowledge or permission.
- Lead to consequences, such as a Denial of Service (DoS) attack or misuse, that the user did not intend to occur. In the case of a DoS attack, the malware — merely by its presence — chokes up memory or network bandwidth. In the case of misuse, the malware deletes, damages, or steals files, or it takes over the entire system.

Viruses, trojans, and worms also differ in significant ways, and these are described in Table 9.1.

Table 9.1

The types of malware, defined

Type of malware	Relationship to host	Self-replicating?	Method of activation
Virus	Must attach itself to a host program or file	Yes, but only by attaching itself to a new host (so infects one computer at a time)	Requires a human action
Trojan	Disguised as an existing or otherwise benign program	No	Activates automatically
Worm	Self-standing code (does not require a host program or file)	Yes (so spreads throughout networks)	Activates automatically

Despite the definitions that Table 9.1 presents, the line between viruses and worms can be blurred, so these terms are sometimes used interchangeably. For example, a virus that is attached to an e-mail message requires the user to open or download that attachment. If the virus then spreads on its own throughout the network, the virus is considered a worm from that point forward. For simplicity's sake, this book will refer to all three types of malware as *viruses* or *malware* and as *trojans* or *worms* only when the distinction is important.

The main sources of infections, from the most frequent to the least, are the following:

- E-mail attachments

  Seemingly innocent attachments remain the major source of viruses. To prevent infections, follow the rules that were outlined in Chapter 8, "Securing E-mail."

- Downloaded software

  It goes without saying that any software downloaded from the Internet is suspicious — even when received from a known and trusted Web site. All executable and binary files should be scanned by antivirus software after downloading and before installation.

- File-sharing services

  With file-sharing services, malware on one computer is only a click away from being copied to another computer. These services include Windows file shares, Samba or Network File System (NFS) running on Linux, instant–messaging clients, and Internet Relay Chat (IRC) clients.

- Floppy disks and CDs

  Prior to the advent of the Internet, such media provided the only means of virus transmission between computer systems. Today, all floppy disks and CDs that contain files copied from another computer — even a familiar one — should still be scanned by antivirus software. For the truly mistrustful, even shrink-wrapped CDs are candidates for antivirus scanning.

- Web sites

  Malicious Web sites and their pop-ups can contain malware in two forms: tiny blank images and HTML tags. The former are invisible on the page but contain spyware, for example, in embedded HTML code. The latter can use your browser to download malicious code from the attacker's Web site to your computer.

- Perimeter attacks

  This new wave of attacks first hit in 2003 with the Blaster worm. For this type of attack, a worm scans ports looking for any available computer on which to perform its dirty tricks. After finding a winner, it helps itself to the computer by downloading itself directly from the attacker's server. So, you could become a victim just by being connected to the Internet — which becomes more and more common with the growth of always-on broadband and T1 lines.

To keep your systems free of these infections, adhere to the following guidelines:

1. Install antivirus software on all clients and servers.
    1.1. Choose only commercial software from reliable vendors, not *warez* or pirated software.
2. Regularly update the software, as often as once or twice a week.
    2.1. Update more frequently during alerts of known virus attacks.
    2.2. Buy an annual subscription package, if available, from the vendor.
3. Check your vendor's Web site every day for virus alerts and consequent emergency updates.
4. Conduct regular scans or set up automatic scans that will occur weekly, at least.
5. Whenever realistic and possible, test any new software on a computer that is not connected to your network. For example, use a segregated development lab that is set up specifically for testing software prior to installation in production environments.
6. Be sure that all employees are taught never to open unknown or unsolicited e-mail attachments, as previously discussed in Chapter 8, "Securing E-mail."
7. Instruct employees to stick to the following process when copying files from a CD or floppy disk:
    7.1. Scan the entire CD or floppy disk.
    7.2. Copy the required files.
        7.2.1. Scan the copied files.
8. If the worst happens, perform the following steps:
    8.1. Clean up by running your antivirus software.
    8.2. Check the software's activity log for details about the attack.
    8.3. Refer to the vendor's Web site for more information about the specific virus.
    8.4. Enter the following information into your own log:
        8.4.1. The date of the incident
        8.4.2. The name of the virus

8.4.3. The number of computers that were attacked

8.4.4. Comments

9. To prevent Web and perimeter attacks, including client-side attacks and cross-site scripting, maintain all browsers in the following manner:

9.1. Install new browser patches as soon as they become available.

9.2. Install antispyware and cookie-removal software, such as Lavasoft Ad-Aware.

9.3. Turn off Microsoft ActiveX controls and active scripting.

9.4. Remove unidentified browser objects that do not have dates or known names.

9.5. Periodically purge the browser history and cookie files. (Because many sites require cookies to function properly, don't disable cookies altogether. Just clean out the stale ones.)

10. Use a firewall to close known ports of attack from trojans and worms.

 Note

Generally, a firewall cannot protect a computer from virus attacks because most viruses operate at the application level (especially when they slip through as e-mail attachments). Similarly, trojans are like mini–application servers that open ports on the victim's computer and then go to town. An application-level firewall or a proxy that strips e-mail attachments can provide some protection. Firewalls will be discussed in more detail in Chapter 11, "Defending Your Network Perimeter."

When you are evaluating antivirus software, look for the following features (listed here in order of importance):

• Offers automatic updates
• Has the ability to perform real-time scanning
• Scans e-mail messages and attachments
• Scans the boot sector

- Provides a scheduler for setting up automated scans
- Allows manual scans
- Detects trojans and worms
- Uses heuristics analysis
- Maintains an activity log
- Provides a quarantine area
- Has the capacity to be deployed on a network

CHAPTER 10

SECURING
YOUR WEB SITE

AS WEB-BASED APPLICATIONS BECOME POPULAR
replacements for client-server applications, the ease of access to
them comes at the price of more security headaches. With the
client-server model, a user must have specific software installed on
his or her workstation to access the application that is on the server.
This model thus restricts access to those that have the particular
client software. With Web applications, on the other hand, anyone
that has a browser and access to the Internet — which, these days,
is basically everyone — can access the application.

When someone visits your Web site, that person is actually visiting your server as a guest. The question is, how hospitable a host
should you be toward your guests? The answer is, you would be too
hospitable if you hadn't properly configured your Web server. The
problem is that such a scenario would allow your Web site to become
anybody's playground — especially that of a malicious hacker.

Web applications can be full of holes. And, as gateways connected to wider systems — including database and application
servers — they can provide doorways that lead straight into company networks. However, these applications can be made reason-
ably secure if you configure them correctly. To do so, you must
accomplish all of the following goals:

- Protecting data and confidential information that resides on the Web site itself
- Preventing malicious manipulation of the application that runs the Web site
- Preventing unauthorized access to the server that hosts the Web application

Securing the Web Site Itself

To protect the contents of your Web site from customers as well as from hackers, maintain the following practices:

1. Never reveal the following:
    1.1. Organizational charts
    1.2. Employee directories
    1.3. Employee phone numbers or e-mail addresses
        1.3.1. Disclose only the main phone number that would be listed in any public phone book.
        1.3.2. Display only generic e-mail addresses, such as *sales@ yourcompany.com* and *support@yourcompany.com*.
    1.4. Internal memos or anything of a confidential nature
    1.5. Maps or schematic diagrams of facility interiors
        1.5.1 Maps and directions to facilities (or links to mapping sites, such as MapQuest and Yahoo!) are fine. This information is publicly available, in any case.

2. Register certain domain names that closely resemble your actual domain name.
    2.1. Register common misspellings and other permutations.
    2.2. In addition, register names that combine your actual domain name with mildly offending or even obscene words. (One example is *yourcompanysucks.com.*) Otherwise, disgruntled employees or others that are critical of your company could beat you to it and post nasty things about the company or even confidential information.
    2.3. Set up the extra domains to automatically redirect users back to your main Web site. That way, even the domains that have offensive names cannot be used against your company.

3. If your site is an e-commerce site, regularly purge all customer credit-card numbers.

   3.1. If possible, purge the credit-card number from your site after the sale clears. Although a repeat customer gains convenience from an already filled-in credit-card number, a hacker gains the knowledge that you're maintaining a database of credit-card numbers to be cracked. (The best practice is to steer clear of maintaining such a database at all. Then again, this practice might not be realistic if your site is heavily trafficked, because the lack of a credit-card database could slow down brisk sales.) Regardless of your setup, hackers don't need to know what that setup is. Require customers to enter their credit-card numbers every time they make a purchase.

Caution

A chilling scenario involves a hacker getting into someone's online account and pretending to make a purchase. If the hacker sees a last name — say, *Smith* — and the last four digits of the credit-card number — say, *xxxx xxxx xxxx 1234* (displayed this way for "protection") — all the hacker needs to do is get into the Web site's database and search for *Smith* and any credit-card number ending in *1234*. Not only can the hacker use the credit-card number elsewhere (beyond your particular Web site), but he or she now has a way into your database for the ultimate booty — a list of all your customers' names and credit-card numbers.

Securing the Web Application

The practices for securing your Web application overlap with those for writing secure programming code, many of which involve detailed technical issues. (For more information, see Chapter 16, "Writing Secure Programming Code," or go to *http://www.owasp.org*, which is the Web site of the Open Web Application Security Project.) To begin, however, you need a general idea of what to look out for, so keep to the rules that the following outline describes:

1. Grant visitors the least amount of privileges.
   1.1. Allow a visitor to access your site only through a guest account which, in turn, belongs to a general group that allows access to the server without a password.
   1.2. Grant visitors only read and execute permissions for Web pages that are publicly visible. Grant no permissions for any other files.

2. If your Web site has a logon screen, follow the password practices that were discussed in Chapter 7, "Putting Software Access Controls in Place."
   2.1. In addition, set up the logon page to use the strongest possible authentication.
      2.1.1. At least 128-bit
      2.1.2. Not Basic authentication, which can easily be sniffed and cracked

3. Set up virtual directories, and don't use the server's root directory as the application's root directory.
   3.1. Each Web application that resides on the server must have its own root directory, which must be distinct from the server's administrative root directory.
   3.2. Place all application-code files, including CGI scripts, into their own virtual subdirectory under the application's root directory. This practice hides the root-directory path.
   3.3. Encrypt all the directories and files that visitors don't need to see.

4. Validate all input from forms on your site — but perform the validation on the server, not on the client.
   4.1. Check for malformed URLs that contain malicious code, especially attempts to call executable files that reside on your system.
   4.2. Avoid writing the validation code in any client-side scripting language, such as JavaScript or Microsoft Visual Basic Scripting Edition (VBScript), because scripting code is embedded in a Web page's HTML code and is thus exposed

to users. Instead, opt for application-level compiled code that resides on the application server.

   4.3. No JavaScript or VBScript shopping carts, because any data (such as a price list) that is embedded in a Web page can easily be manipulated and sent back to the server.

5. Do not allow source code (especially include files) to contain confidential server information.

   5.1. No IDs

   5.2. No passwords

   5.3. No database connection strings

   5.4. No version or application information

6. Hide error messages and stack traces by redirecting the page to a generic error page that does not display any details.

   6.1. Error messages are confusing to nontechnical users but can provide crucial information to attackers that have criminal intentions. For example, application names and versions or server information can inform an attacker of a useful vulnerability.

7. To send form data, try to use the POST rather than the GET attribute of the HTML <form> tag.

   7.1. If the application requires you to use GET, encrypt the query strings — especially those that contain cookie and session ID information. The encryption will prevent URL spoofing and session-replay attacks in the future.

   7.2. Do not use GET to send logon information — under any circumstances.

   7.3. Use redirection or domain masking to hide and mask URLs that contain query strings.

8. Secure your database servers just like you do other application servers.

   8.1. Restrict access to only the data that is needed to process a form.

   8.2. Keep patches up-to-date.

   8.3. Remove unneeded services and accounts.

9. If your site requires users to log on, block deep linking.

   9.1. Don't allow users to bypass your logon page and go directly to any other page that your site contains. If a user attempts to do so by typing a URL into the browser's address bar or by clicking any link, redirect that user to your logon page.

9.2. Include code on each child page that checks whether the user has logged on. If he or she hasn't done so, the code should force that user back to the logon screen.

9.3. Note that sessions can still be hijacked and spoofed even if each child page contains validation code. A hacker can sniff a logon page after it has been submitted and replay its validation code. So, another method of checking the user's logon information is including the validation code in the underlying code that is located on the server. Because this code is invisible to users, it can't be detected by sniffers. (The bottom line: however you do it, block deep linking.)

10. Audit code for security defects.

10.1. SQL injection strings

10.2. Buffer overflows

10.3. Malformed URLs

11. If your site uses any Web services, protect traffic and data.

11.1. Encrypt all traffic to and from Web services.

11.2. Validate all user input contained in XML files that are sent by Web services.

Securing the Web Server

The security of your Web server is intimately tied to the security of your underlying network. Because a Web server is no different from any other network server (except that it contains software for displaying Web pages), a strong Web server can't make up for a poorly configured network. Therefore, keep in mind that the rules for Web servers that are outlined here are related to the network issues that are discussed in Chapter 11, "Defending Your Network Perimeter."

1. Take care that your Web server is a dedicated server and that it is located within the DMZ section of your firewall. (The DMZ

configuration is explained in Chapter 11, "Defending Your Network Perimeter.")

   1.1. This configuration protects your internal network from any
breaches of the Web server, and it protects your Web server
from any hostile Internet traffic.

   1.2. You should harden the Web server like any other application server or bastion host.

2. Enable auditing and turn on logging for periodic review.

   2.1. Check for unusual or modified URLs, which can indicate
unauthorized attempts to access your server.

   2.2. Write scripts that monitor your Web and application logs for
URL modifications. Run the scripts as often as necessary,
based on the volume of traffic to the site.

3. Delete or turn off unnecessary applications and services.

   3.1. Delete sample Web pages, such as those that come with
Microsoft Internet Information Services (IIS) and Apache
Web server.

   3.2. Delete sample scripts, such as Perl CGI scripts, that come
packaged with the server. Hackers are wise to these and
can use them as points of entry.

   3.3. On IIS, unmap ISAPI DLLs. On Apache Web server, unin-
stall mods.

   3.4. Delete default accounts or change their passwords. Hackers
have lists of these.

4. Disable the ability to list or browse directories.

   4.1. This feature would simply provide a hacker with information about your Web site's directory structure.

   4.2. Replace any URL that is used for directory browsing with a
generic index page that does not contain any server clues.

5. On Apache Web server, avoid using the .htacess file for direc-
tory-level security because an attacker could replace or easily
crack this file.

   5.1. Instead, use the server's own ACL system to set permissions
for access to sensitive Web pages.

6. Remove or modify all server banners.

   6.1. Note that IIS and Apache Web server each have a banner
that identifies the server name and version.

    6.2. Make the banner blank or insert misleading information —
as a decoy to throw off a potential hacker.

7. Disable reverse proxy settings.
    7.1. A reverse proxy defeats the purpose of a proxy and reveals
the IP addresses that are inside a private network.

8. For e-commerce transactions, use a certificate authority and
Secure Sockets Layer (SSL).
    8.1. SSL encrypts sensitive traffic, such as names, addresses, order
information, and credit-card numbers.
    8.2. Remember that users can set their browsers to check for
legitimate certificates and to prevent the display of spoofed
or malicious sites that don't have an official seal.

9. Separate the development environment from the QA environment
by assigning them to different servers.
    9.1. Furthermore, segregate these environments from all produc-
tion servers.
    9.2. Make the production servers inaccessible to developers.

10. Monitor your Web site for defacement.
    10.1. Be aware that defacement is now the rage simply because
it's easy. All an attacker needs to do is hack into a Web
server and then replace one of the Web pages that reside
there.
    10.2. Besides periodically checking the Web site itself, monitor
your access logs for unauthorized FTP access that origi-
nated outside the network.

11. Install an Intrusion Detection System (IDS) such as Tripwire,
which monitors your Web server and conducts regular penetration tests.
    11.1. Firewalls block traffic, whereas IDSs alert you to trouble.
They're the cyberspace equivalent of burglar alarms.

CHAPTER 11

DEFENDING YOUR NETWORK PERIMETER

SO FAR, THIS BOOK HAS DISCUSSED SECURING your internal network. Now, you need to step outside the boundaries of your network and guard the gates around your castle. In other words, you need to defend the perimeter of your network — and beyond.

However, remember that perimeter defense and internal security are tightly bound. A strong perimeter defense — "I use a firewall, so I'm safe" — without strong internal security equals security suicide. Think about this: A country that maintained great border guards at its frontier but no police force inside the country would be totally dependent on its border strength. If an attacker got through the border, there would be no stopping of damage to interior cities. Similarly, the secret to defending your network is *defense in depth*, which means marrying perimeter defense with internal security. In other words, you need hardware firewalls at the perimeter of your network (outside) as well as software firewalls on your host computer (inside).

Note

Another way to think about defense in depth is as a layered approach that is like an onion skin. Each time a hacker peels away one layer, the next eye-stinging layer is exposed, and then another, and another — each more caustic than the last — until, finally, the hacker is forced to put the onion down.

This chapter does focus specifically on your perimeter-defense plan, and because firewalls are the major players in perimeter defense, they are the major subjects of this chapter. However, the chapter provides a checklist of items that your perimeter-defense plan should cover, rather than the narrow details of firewall configuration. Perimeter defense involves more than such configuration — it includes optimally placing firewalls within the boundaries of your network, choosing among the available types of firewalls, setting up your firewalls in an architecture configuration, knowing the strengths and weaknesses of firewalls in general, and effectively combining firewalls with other security tools.

Before you even set up your perimeter defense, you need to segregate your network in the following manner:

1. Isolate your network servers according to the following roles:
   1.1. Functional area, such as accounting or marketing
   1.2. Strategic IT asset, such as a Web, database, or application server

2. Wall off each server by giving it the following items of its own:
   2.1. A subnet that is isolated within the network
   2.2. A router, or gateway
   2.3. A firewall or firewall combination, such as a DMZ for strategic IT assets

3. Segregate your assets by "threat versus value," according to the assessment that you created in Chapter 3, "Assessing Your System."

Note

A *router* is a scaled-down computer that forwards network and IP traffic to other computers. A router segregates network sections and offers some protection by hiding a client's identity. A *firewall* is a type of router that checks traffic and blocks it, if necessary, before forwarding it.

After you've mapped out the segregation of your network, you can set up your firewalls according to the following details:

1. Firewall placement: possible locations from the outside moving inward
    1.1. In border routers at the edge of your network, where the network interfaces with the Internet or a wide area network (WAN)
    1.2. In interior routers that move traffic from the border into your network
    1.3. In a DMZ, which is a set of routers that surround your strategic IT assets
    1.4. In separate routers or router combinations that each enclose a segregated portion of your network
    1.5. In software firewalls on all the individual workstations

2. Firewall types: advantages and disadvantages
    2.1. Software
        2.1.1. Packet filtering (used by Zone Labs ZoneAlarm, Black Ice Software BlackICE PC Protection, netfilter/iptables, and Internet Connection Firewall in Windows XP)
            2.1.1.1. Blocks only network protocols, based on port number and protocol type
            2.1.1.2. Examines only the headers of TCP packets
            2.1.1.3. Checks packets once in each direction without preserving state information, so "forgets" the packet source
            2.1.1.4. Being stateless, can't block outgoing requests or incoming malicious code

2.1.1.5. Can't defend against spoofed packets or attacks that use malformed packets

2.1.1.6. Makes for the fastest firewall because packet filtering does not interfere with server functions, which would degrade performance

2.1.1.7. Provides a quick and easy installation

2.1.1.8. Used best on workstations or individual client computers rather than on network servers

2.1.2. Stateful packet inspection

2.1.2.1. Examines packet headers and bodies, so can check application types and block those that are suspected of carrying malicious code.

2.1.2.2. Preserves state, so checks whether an incoming packet matches an outgoing request. (This type of firewall can thus block a trojan, for example, that tries to send data back to a malicious host that never sent an incoming request.)

2.1.2.3. Combines the speed of packet filtering with protection against malicious applications, so is the most popular type of firewall.

2.2. Hardware

2.2.1. Application-layer (such as Squid and Cisco PIX Firewalls)

2.2.1.1. Consists of a dedicated server that acts as a proxy between a trusted (internal) network and any number of untrusted (Internet or other external) networks.

2.2.1.2. Hides clients that are inside your network by breaking the connection between a client and the external network, and creating a fresh connection between itself and the external network. The connection appears to be coming from the proxy server rather than the actual, requesting client.

2.2.1.3. May degrade performance due to the extra hop through the proxy.

2.2.1.4. Requires a separate server for each TCP protocol:

2.2.1.4.1. HTTP (Web)

2.2.1.4.2. SMTP (e-mail)

2.2.1.4.3. DNS (naming)

2.2.1.4.4. SSH (remote shell)

2.2.1.5. Needs to be hardened like any other server:

2.2.1.5.1. Unneeded services disabled

2.2.1.5.2. Unneeded accounts removed

2.2.1.5.3. Access restricted

2.2.1.6. Known by other names:

2.2.1.6.1. Dual-homed host

2.2.1.6.2. Bastion host

2.2.1.6.3. Proxy gateway

2.2.1.6.4. Proxy server

2.2.1.7. Still susceptible to DoS attacks and able to be hacked like any other network server.

2.2.1.8. When improperly configured so that certain types of port forwarding are allowed, opens the door directly into the private network and functions as well as no firewall at all.

2.2.2. Circuit-level

2.2.2.1. Works in a similar manner as an application-layer proxy does, but opens a dedicated channel (circuit) between the requesting client and the receiving, external server

2.2.2.2. Requires specialized software — which uses the SOCKS protocol — on clients and gateways

2.2.2.3. Might not examine packets at the application level, thus allowing malicious code to pass

3. Firewall architecture configurations: possible setups in order of increasing strength

3.1. Screening router — a router that acts as a firewall by using one of the following types of software:

3.1.1. Packet filtering

        3.1.2. Network Address Translation (NAT)
            3.1.2.1. Merely hides internal network IP addresses
            3.1.2.2. Creates security by anonymity, but not a true firewall

  3.2. Bastion host — a proxy server that contains two network cards: one connected to the internal network and another connected to the external network

      3.2.1. As an application-layer firewall, uses port forwarding

      3.2.2. Hides the interior network like NAT does

      3.2.3. Must be hardened like any other server

  3.3. Screened host — a combination of a screening router and a bastion host

      3.3.1. The screening router is exposed to the external network.

      3.3.2. The bastion host is exposed to the internal network.

      3.3.3. Incoming requests are filtered by the screening router and then by the bastion host before coming in.

      3.3.4. Outgoing requests go through the bastion host to the screening router and then out.

  3.4. Screened subnet (also known as a DMZ) — two screening routers with one or more bastion hosts that sit between them

      3.4.1. All application servers (Web servers, e-mail servers, and so on) are hardened as bastion hosts and placed between the screening routers.

      3.4.2. The application servers are exposed to the Internet but not to the internal network, and the internal network can access the application servers.

4. Firewall rules: establishing which traffic to allow by employing a user interface on the firewall server or by modifying configuration files

  4.1. The parameters you need, at a bare minimum:

      4.1.1. The protocol type

      4.1.2. The source address and port

      4.1.3. The destination address and port

4.1.4. The non-TCP applications to allow (or block)

4.1.5. The direction of the request (incoming or outgoing)

4.1.6. The action to be taken when the rule is met

    4.1.6.1. Allow

    4.1.6.2. Reject

    4.1.6.4. Deny (reject, but transmit a message to the sender)

4.1.7. The action to be taken for all other traffic (everything that is not explicitly allowed or rejected)

    4.1.7.1. Deny (the action you should set as the default)

4.2. The TCP protocols that you should set rules for:

    4.2.1. HTTP (Web)

    4.2.2. SMTP (e-mail)

    4.2.3. DNS (naming)

    4.2.4. SSH (remote shell)

    4.2.5. ICMP echo (ping)

    4.2.6. FTP (File Transfer Protocol) and TFTP (Trivial File Transfer Protocol)

    4.2.7. Telnet

    4.2.8. Finger

    4.2.9. SNMP (Simple Network Management Protocol)

    4.2.10. Windows file sharing using NetBIOS

    4.2.11. NNTP (news)

    4.2.12. Other, lesser-known protocols in the TCP suite that your applications require

 Tip

When setting DNS rules, be sure to prohibit zone transfers so that IP redirection is prevented. When setting ICMP echo rules, be sure to hide your server from pinging, which causes Ping of Death DoS attacks.

Important ————————————————————————————

> Base your choices of firewall types, architecture configurations, and firewall rules on the relative vulnerabilities and values of your IT assets. This can't be repeated enough. First comes the design of your IT security policy, followed by the design of your firewalls, followed by the implementation of your firewalls.

The strengths and weaknesses of firewalls are the following:

1. Strengths
   1.1. Provide a single point of access that can be securely monitored and protected
   1.2. Manage and log traffic from external sources
   1.3. Enforce your security policy
2. Weaknesses
   2.1. Can't protect against social engineering or insider attacks
   2.2. Can't compensate for poor policy, weak network architecture, or other security holes
   2.3. Can't protect against a flawed application that the rules allow in
   2.4. Can't bar traffic to the internal network that is brought in through unauthorized access, which the following cause to take place:
      2.4.1. Modems on the internal network that dial out, bypassing the firewall and bringing in unchecked (untrusted) external traffic
      2.4.2. Wireless access points on the internal network, which have the same net effect as modems do
      2.4.3. Other remote access software, such as Unix X Windows and Unix 'r' services
      2.4.4. Access that originates outside a virtual private network (VPN)

Important

Set up all remote users on VPNs that connect to the internal network through a border firewall.

Firewalls provide a passive defense. They simply guard the gates without advising you of any trouble. To supplement their functionality, you need an active defense — which is provided by a set of Intrusion Detection Systems (IDSs) — to complete the circle. An IDS acts as a burglar alarm that rings when a network attack is in progress. For example, an IDS can alert a system administrator that something is amiss with your network traffic. IDSs make up a subject of their own that is covered in Chapter 12, "Detecting Intrusions."

Another passive defense that firewalls provide is logging, which is the recording of all network activity, malicious or otherwise. You should always turn on the logging features that your firewalls provide, if they are not already turned on by default. (Note that IDSs can also log information.) Logs can be configured in a variety of ways but, at a minimum, they should record the following:

- Client and destination names and IP addresses
- Authentication status
- Time stamp
- Protocol name
- Protocol command (for example, HTTP GET or POST)
- Result code

To complete your perimeter defense, always combine firewalls with the following:

- Antivirus software
- Content-filtering software (blocks spam and offensive material)
- A series of IDSs
- Physical security

CHAPTER 12

DETECTING INTRUSIONS

INTRUSION DETECTION REQUIRES SENTRIES WHO watch for trouble at the gates and messengers who present reports to the castle owner. However, Intrusion Detection Systems (IDSs) — which act in both capacities — supply just one part of an overall intrusion-detection strategy. To effectively detect intrusions, you must perform the following steps:

1. Complete a security audit.
2. Conduct a penetration test.
3. Install IDSs.

 Note

Keep in mind that the other side of the intrusion-detection coin is *incident response*. Whereas intrusion detection entails prevention and review, incident response concerns capture and enforcement. Chapter 13, "Responding to Incidents," covers the enforcement side.

It is important to complete the intrusion-detection steps in order. The security audit essentially involves a policy review. Although it is listed separately, the penetration test — which simulates hackers trying to breach your IT systems — can be viewed as part of the security audit. It is listed separately due to its technical and hands-on nature, as opposed to the policy-review orientation of the security audit.

You should perform the security audit first and the penetration test second to prevent any distortion of network activity that could affect the audit results. After you have completed both, you can configure your IDSs to target your network's weakest points.

Before imparting the details of the intrusion-detection steps, this chapter will acquaint you with the steps that compose a hack attack cycle. These steps are presented in order in the following outline:

1. Scout the terrain.
   1.1. Review the company's (or individual victim's) Web site for clues and public information.
   1.2. Obtain the company's DNS and IP-address information.
      1.2.1. Make use of nslookup and ping (tools that are shipped with both Linux and Windows) as well as hacking tools that are less standard.
      1.2.2. Perform an online search of the WHOIS databases and the ARIN (American Registry for Internet Numbers) database.
   1.3. Scan the range of IP addresses by running Nmap or another network scanner or probe.
   1.4. Ascertain which operating systems are being used, and try to map the network architecture.
   1.5. Draw on social-engineering methods to supplement the previously found information.
      1.5.1. Steal passwords, and obtain network information.
      1.5.2. Drop a trojan on one or more workstations or servers to acquire the same.
2. Plan the attack.
   2.1. Inventory the following:
      2.1.1. Operating systems and their version numbers

      2.1.2   Open ports and the applications that are running on them

      2.1.3   Network structure, including the placement of routers and firewalls

  2.2. Set up a packet sniffer — Ethereal or tcpdump — to actively scan live traffic.

      2.2.1. Be on the lookout for unencrypted passwords and other tidbits in exposed traffic.

      2.2.2. Sift the data for information about any TCP protocols that can be exploited.

  2.3. Research the following by using Google or by exploring hackers' Web sites:

      2.3.1. Known vulnerabilities of any items in the previously created inventory.

      2.3.2. Newsgroup postings that were made by anyone in the company and that contain either security information or tidbits that can be combined into such information.

      2.3.3. Passwords or holes that prior intruders have posted on Web sites. (You'd be surprised at the amount of groundwork that might already have been laid.)

  2.4. Check the vendors' Web sites for the following information:

      2.4.1. Known vulnerabilities of the particular product versions that the previously created inventory contains

      2.4.2. Default configurations and passwords that were set at the factory

3. Begin the attack.

  3.1. Penetrate the system by directly exploiting the previously found vulnerabilities.

  3.2. Indirectly attack the system from an already compromised third-party server.

  3.3. Crash the gates by exploiting any border-router or firewall vulnerabilities.

  3.4. Hide any evidence of forced entry by manipulating or deleting logs.

4. Escalate privileges.

  4.1. Be aware that your initial attack might have occurred on a server that belongs to an unimportant group.

4.2. Try to gain root privileges on a Unix system or administrator privileges on a Windows system.

4.3. Keep in mind that the goal is to move from single-user access to complete control of the entire system.

4.4. If your goal is a DoS attack, bring the system down.

5. Leave a calling card.

5.1. Again, hide any evidence by manipulating or deleting logs.

5.2. Install a back door — your own secret account or a trojan tool — so you can come back to the candy store whenever your sweet tooth flares up.

Keeping the hack attack cycle in mind, you can begin your security audit, which this entire book can essentially be used as a checklist for. The following outline thus presents a distillation of the other chapters, enhanced with specifically audit-oriented material, into the highlights of an audit game plan:

1. Audit design and planning

1.1. Decide on the frequency of audits.

1.1.1. Annually or monthly, depending on the frequency of changes in your environment

1.1.2. Whenever a major business change or IT architecture change occurs

1.2. Establish the scope of an audit.

1.2.1. The IT (and related) staff to interview

1.2.2 The data to collect

1.2.3. The paperwork to review

1.3. Choose who will conduct the audit and participate in it.

1.3.1. A third-party company?

1.3.2. Inside management and staff?

1.4. Determine the duration of the audit.

1.4.1. Depends on the size of your organization

1.4.2. Requires a minimum of one week for visits, interviews, and data collection

2. Audit process

2.1. Review your security policy.

2.1.1. Look at the age of your policy and the frequency of updates to it.

  2.1.2. Evaluate your policy for consistency.
    2.1.2.1. With practices that are standard in the industry
    2.1.2.2. With your company's actual, on-site practices

2.2. Review your security management.
  2.2.1. Take a look at an overview of the structure and composition of your IT security department.
  2.2.2. Examine the procedures that occur along your chain of command for communicating security-related matters to employees.

2.3. Review your personnel management:
  2.3.1. Hiring and firing practices
  2.3.2. Security-awareness training
  2.3.3. Supervision of employees on the job

2.4. Review your physical security by inspecting your facilities.
  2.4.1. Evaluate your physical access controls.
  2.4.2. Look for possible vulnerabilities in the layout of your facilities.

2.5. Review your disaster-recovery and backup procedures:
  2.5.1. Business-continuity plans to avoid downtime of business or critical systems
  2.5.2. The way that data is backed up when a hacking or natural disaster occurs
  2.5.3. Recovery procedures that occur after a disaster

2.6. Review your access-control procedures.
  2.6.1. Look at the types of your access controls.
  2.6.2. Compare your policies with your practices for allowing access and setting up groups.
  2.6.3. Evaluate your hierarchy of groups and the group memberships.
  2.6.4. Check the validity of each account and determine whether it should remain active.
  2.6.5. Assess the access level (for example, user versus administrator) of each valid account.

2.7. Review your network-security and Internet practices.
  2.7.1. Perform a complete scan of your network.
  2.7.2. Create a diagram of your entire network.

2.7.3. Compare your security policy with actual employee practices.

2.7.4. Scan for unauthorized access from the following sources:

    2.7.4.1. Unauthorized wireless access points

    2.7.4.2. Rogue Web servers and sites

    2.7.4.3. Unauthorized modems

    2.7.4.4. Abuse of VPN access

    2.7.4.5. Unauthorized instant-messaging software

2.7.5. Search for pirated or unauthorized downloads of software, music, or offensive material.

2.7.6. Go over your Internet policy, including who is allowed to access the Internet and the specific sites that are permitted.

2.7.7. Assess the effectiveness of your firewall architecture and firewall rules.

2.7.8. Evaluate your practices regarding antivirus software, including the frequency of updates and the effectiveness of your practices.

3. Audit report

  3.1. Write a final product that includes the following:

    3.1.1. Vulnerability assessments of assets that are ranked by importance

    3.1.2. Possible courses of action to mitigate threats and vulnerabilities

    3.1.3. Network diagrams that include points of concern

    3.1.4. A review of weaknesses that need to be addressed and recommendations for their resolution

Now that you've completed the soft and squishy part of your intrusion-detection strategy, it's time to have some real fun: the simulated hack attack — otherwise known as the penetration test. The basic components of this test are the following:

- Research
- Scan
- Sniff
- Spoof

- Break in
- Report

Note

Appendix C, "Tools of the Trade," contains a complete list — including URLs for downloading — of the software that any hacker-fighting toolkit should contain. The outline of the penetration test that appears momentarily instructs you to run a number of these tools.

The penetration test requires you to examine several areas, which together incorporate all of the just-listed penetration-test components, as the following outline describes:

1. Physical security
   1.1. Check the obvious (for example, open or unlocked doors).
   1.2. Test the ease of bypassing access controls by piggybacking or sneaking past guards.
   1.3. Look for mechanical flaws in card-key or other access-control systems.

2. Social engineering
   2.1. Check the ease of applying social-engineering methods to gain passwords, network information, and other ways in.
      2.1.1. Make as many calls as needed to gather small pieces of information.

3. Company information
   3.1. Review your company's Web site for any vulnerabilities that can be researched.
   3.2. Be creative: Check the job listings on your Web site or in the newspaper for IT positions with your company. Because these positions require specific technical skills, job listings frequently contain details about systems and applications.
   3.3. Do some homework by making use of Google:
      3.3.1. Search for newsgroup postings from anyone in your company.
      3.3.2. Research the company and its IT infrastructure.

       3.3.3. Perform WHOIS and ARIN queries to obtain the following information:
          3.3.3.1. The blocks of IP addresses that belong to your company
          3.3.3.2. The company's DNS server names and IP addresses

4. Network mapping
   4.1. Perform a complete port scan of the previously found IP addresses by using Nmap or another port scanner.
   4.2. Make a complete list of the following:
      4.2.1. Open ports
      4.2.2. The services that are running on those ports
      4.2.3. Server types:
         4.2.3.1. E-mail (SMTP)
         4.2.3.2. Web (HTTP)
         4.2.3.3. Naming (DNS)
         4.2.3.4. Other application, such as IBM Lotus Domino
      4.2.4. Operating systems
      4.2.5. Firewall information
         4.2.5.1. Dedicated proxy servers
         4.2.5.2. Packet-filtering firewalls
   4.3. Poke and prod for server holes by using Netcat, which is the hacking equivalent of Telnet on steroids.
   4.4. Check for a variety of other server vulnerabilities by running Nessus.
   4.5. See whether your network is susceptible to DNS spoofing or IP flooding.
      4.5.1. Try spoofing or manipulating packets by using one or more tools such as Ettercap.
      4.5.2. See whether it is possible to send spoofed e-mail messages using SMTP.
      4.5.3. Check the integrity of packets and see whether you can pass unencrypted, confidential information through your network by using Ethereal or another packet sniffer.

4.6. Scan for wireless access points by running NetStumbler or Kismet.

4.7. Look for extraneous remote-access connections (and test for leakage and encryption strength, if appropriate):

    4.7.1. Dial-in systems

    4.7.2. Modems

    4.7.3. VPN connections

5. Web servers

    5.1. When performing port scans, pay close attention to your Web servers.

    5.2. Use Nikto (a popular Web-scanning tool) to check for the following vulnerabilities in your Web pages:

        5.2.1. CGI scripts written in Perl or any other scripting language

        5.2.2. ActiveX controls

        5.2.3. Applets written in the Sun Java programming language

        5.2.4. Poorly crafted HTML code

        5.2.5. Invalid digital certificates

    5.3. Test your input validation by attempting to pass malformed URLs and query strings.

    5.4. Perform load testing, which checks performance as well as the load that a server can handle.

        5.4.1. Load testing also checks the likelihood of impacts from DoS attacks.

 Tip

In what is known as a *man-in-the-middle attack*, a hacker intercepts a valid digital certificate and replaces it with one that appears like the original. The hacker then takes advantage of the phony certificate to steal passwords and account information through the Internet. You should therefore keep your certificates up-to-date and purchase them only from known and reliable certificate authorities, such as VeriSign.

6. Databases
   6.1. Check the ease of accessing your databases from your Web sites and Web applications and from other clients.
   6.2. See whether input from SQL queries is validated to prevent malicious code injection.
   6.3. Verify that neither user IDs nor passwords from ODBC (Open Database Connectivity) or other database drivers are exposed in source code.

7. Viruses, spam, and spyware
   7.1. Run complete scans for the following:
      7.1.1. Viruses, trojans, and worms (by running antivirus software)
      7.1.2. Spyware (by running advertisement blocking-and-removing software)
      7.1.3. Spam (by running spam-filtering software)
   7.2. If you have any Unix or Linux systems, run chkrootkit to ferret out rootkits.

8. Passwords
   8.1. Check the ease of bypassing your password and operating-system access controls.
   8.2. See whether your password files — encrypted, hashed, or not — can be accessed.
      8.2.1. If so, run John the Ripper or L0phtCrack to test the strength of the passwords.

9. Routers and firewalls
   9.1. Check for holes and misconfigurations:
      9.1.1. Are default passwords and settings still in place?
      9.1.2. When performing port scans, can these devices be remotely accessed too easily?

10. All vulnerabilities
    10.1. Prepare a report that contains the following:
       10.1.1. A list of the vulnerabilities that you discovered with detailed documentation about each one
       10.1.2. A numerical ranking for the seriousness of each vulnerability
       10.1.3. Recommendations for closing the open holes

Important

The previous outline presents the essential steps of a complete and thorough penetration test. These steps should be attempted only with the written consent of your company's management personnel, who must understand that the testing process could cause network outages but will occur during off-peak hours (late at night or on weekends). If you choose to hire third-party penetration testers, be sure that your company's legal counsel also reviews and approves the test.

Rules for Contracting Third-Party Penetration Testers

Hiring a consulting company to conduct your penetration test is like plunging a two-edged sword inside your network: You give the network the independent appraisal that it should receive, but you also trust outsiders with your network secrets. Nightmare scenario: Incompetent consultants bestow a clean bill of health on your network but miss a gaping hole. Worse scenario: The consultants find a gaping hole but bestow a clean bill of health and sell your secrets to a hacker or competitor (maybe even splitting the loot with the buyer that they've found).

To avoid protection rackets and other unsavory tactics, perform the following honesty checks on any so-called security consulting company:

- Find out how long the company has been in business for.
- Look over the company's Web site.
- Request a client list with references. (If the company won't produce either, be suspicious.)
- Verify all references as well as all current and former clients.
- Check with the Better Business Bureau for any complaints that have been filed against the company.
- Get the names of the company officers and verify their biographies.
- Conduct resume and background checks on the particular staff members that the company assigns to you.

Now that you know the weak points of your network, you can post the sentries in their watchtowers and the messengers at their stations. In other words, you can install IDSs according to the following outline, remembering that their usage and placement should be driven by the rankings of values, threats, and vulnerabilities from the earlier assessment of your IT assets:

1. IDS detection types
   1.1. Anomaly-based
      1.1.1. Uses a baseline of normal (expected) network activity
      1.1.2. Watches for irregular activity: traffic spikes during normally quiet hours and unexpected traffic on certain types of servers
      1.1.3. Remains susceptible to false positive readings
      1.1.4. Does not require updates for new attack types
      1.1.5. Rarely turns up in the IDS products that are currently available
   1.2. Signature-based
      1.2.1. Uses rules (like the signatures in antivirus software) to look for targeted attacks.
      1.2.2. Requires you to update a rules file with new attacks and attack methods.
      1.2.3. Contains lists of the patterns and expressions that are found in malicious code (such as the malformed and bizarre URLs that hack attacks are full of). The rules try to match these patterns and expressions against incoming and outgoing traffic.
      1.2.4. Allows you to set the rules to also check for the following:
         1.2.4.1. Scouting, such as port scanning and sniffing
         1.2.4.2. Multiple attempts at logging on or a failed attempt
         1.2.4.3. An excessive traffic load (which might indicate a DoS attack)
      1.2.5. Commonly appears in IDS products

2. IDS location types
   2.1. Host-based
      2.1.1. Necessitates installation on an individual host
      2.1.2. Protects only that one host
      2.1.3. Requires the host to have a network card in non-promiscuous mode for its dedicated network traffic
   2.2. Network-based
      2.2.1. Necessitates installation on a network segment that is located between hosts
      2.2.2. Examines traffic on that network segment
      2.2.3. Hooks into a network card in promiscuous mode to capture all the traffic that passes through the segment (rather than only the traffic that is directed to its neighboring hosts)
   2.3. Distributed
      2.3.1. Entails remote installation with central control.
      2.3.2. Allows you to set up a complex architecture.
      2.3.3. Uses network cards that are promiscuous and/or nonpromiscuous. The type of each card is based on the location of the network segment and the type of traffic that the IDS is attempting to detect there. No black-and-white rules exist.

3. IDS alert methods
   3.1. Paging or sending an e-mail message to a system administrator
   3.2. Saving a log entry that contains the following:
      3.2.1. A date-and-time stamp
      3.2.2. The source and destination IP addresses and ports
      3.2.3. The protocol name or type
   3.3. Logging an entry in the Windows NT Event Viewer or the Unix syslog
      3.3.1. If you choose this method, designate one server as the standard time bearer and keep the clocks throughout the network synchronized with that server. As a result, all the time stamps that appear in the log will be consistent and able to be meaningfully compared.

3.4. Sending a message (possibly by means of SNMP, which has its own weaknesses, however) to a management console

4. Post-alert courses of action
4.1. Closing the session to stop the suspicious traffic
4.2. Copying the raw packets to a text file and archiving the file for later inspection
4.3. Updating your firewall rules to block the offending traffic

5. Factors in IDS selection
5.1. The ease of being evaded (discussed momentarily)
5.2. The ability to withstand heavy network traffic versus pooping out when bombarded
5.3. Scalability and adaptability to network changes and growth
5.4. The alert methods that you can choose among
5.5. The maximum number of rules that are supported
5.6. The frequency at which you will need to update the rules and the ease of installing these updates

6. Schemes that hackers employ to evade IDSs
6.1. Fragmenting packets so the IDS can't reassemble them exactly as they were sent
6.2. Performing slow port scans that are longer than the IDS horizon, say hourly rather than every second
6.3. Spoofing IP addresses to hide the hacker's origin, or bouncing an attack off a proxy or other third-party server that the hacker has already compromised
6.4. Taking advantage of services on unexpected ports (such as a Web server on a port other than 80), which the IDS doesn't expect
6.5. Applying multiple patterns to attack scripts to avoid the IDS rules

 Note

The content of IDS rules is beyond the scope of this book. However, you should regularly review your rules for accuracy, efficiency, and their ability to withstand network loads.

You might be thinking that an IDS sounds exactly like a firewall. Well, a firewall blocks traffic and might also log traffic. An IDS does not block traffic but does log traffic. If anything, an IDS resembles a network sniffer (Ethereal or tcpdump) because an IDS examines all the packets that pass through it. In fact, you can run the output of an IDS through Ethereal and then examine it.

 Important

> IDSs act as backups to firewalls — never as their replacements. Firewalls are a must, whereas IDSs are optional — and unreliable.

Now, what if the worst happens despite all your hard work and bulletproof planning? That will be covered next.

CHAPTER 13

RESPONDING TO INCIDENTS

CYBERPIRATES HAVE TAKEN YOUR COMPUTER ship hostage. In other words, you've been hacked. The unexpected, the unplanned, what you've worked against and hoped would never happen has finally happened. Now what do you do? The answer is that you regain control of your computer ship and clean up the mess that the cyberpirates made. In other words, you carry out your *incident-response process*, which consists of the following steps:

1. Create an incident-response plan
2. Put ongoing attack-detection processes in motion
3. Stop an attack as soon as it has been detected
4. Preserve evidence of the attack
5. Notify the appropriate parties of the attack
6. Take corrective action

When Is an Incident an Incident?

In addition to classic hack attacks, the following abuses of your IT system are considered *incidents*:

- A network intrusion that originates outside your network
- Any disruption or slowing down of your network activity (possible DoS attack)
- Unauthorized access (physical or virtual) of any IT system
- Theft or alteration of any data, computer file, or intellectual property
- Inappropriate use of the Internet
- Storage of a personal, inappropriate, or illegal file on a company computer
- Unauthorized installation of software
- Sending or receiving spam or any inappropriate e-mail message
- Detection of a virus or worm
- Sending or receiving a hoax

Keep in mind that even a single compromise on an unimportant system can be escalated to full control of your entire network. For that reason, you should immediately remedy any incident that appears to be a minor attack.

Creating an Incident-Response Plan

To create a successful incident-response plan, perform the following steps:

1. Choose the members of your incident-response team, which should be cross-departmental (technical and nontechnical).
   1.1. Senior management
      1.1.1. Because the success of any incident-response effort can be driven only from the top, senior management's key function is supporting such an effort.
      1.1.2. However, you don't need to drag senior management into every incident; the seriousness of the incident governs whether and in what capacity you should

notify them. For example, you don't need to inform them about a single employee who is storing pornography on his or her hard disk, but if the same employee is running an illegal child-pornography ring, that's another matter. Furthermore, if a particular incident might cause business losses, or it noticeably disrupts network traffic, senior management needs to know.

  1.2. Human-resources personnel

      1.2.1. Because an incident could signify an insider attack, or it might involve the improper use of IT property by an employee, the human-resources department must be represented.

  1.3. Information-security workers

      1.3.1. These people comprise your frontline troops, so they must always be part of any incident-response team.

  1.4. Technical staff members who have expertise in the following areas:

      1.4.1. Networking

      1.4.2. Routers

      1.4.3. Programming

      1.4.4. Database administration

      1.4.5. System administration

      1.4.6. Internet technologies

  1.5. External people

      1.5.1. Law-enforcement personnel

      1.5.2. Third-party support staff

2. Describe how incidents should be reported.

  2.1. Designate a single point of contact for incident reporting (because maintaining an authorized contact point prevents the spread of rumors, panic, and hoaxes).

      2.1.1. Phone number or e-mail address that is available 24/7 and that reaches someone on the incident-response team who is on call

  2.2. Ask for the following information in each incident report (which can also be made available to employees as an online form on the corporate intranet or as a printed form):

      2.2.1. The date and time of the incident

2.2.2. The individual who is reporting the incident
    2.2.2.1. Name
    2.2.2.2. Telephone number
    2.2.2.3. E-mail address
    2.2.2.4. Department or location
2.2.3. The physical location of the incident
2.2.4. A list of the computer systems that have been affected
2.2.5. A description of the incident and how it was detected
2.2.6. The location of any evidence and how that evidence is being stored and handled

3. Define the levels of response.
  3.1. Define a hierarchy of possible incidents, prioritizing them by their seriousness levels.
  3.2. For each incident level, decide which organizational levels should be notified and which team members should participate in the response.
    3.2.1. Create a list of escalation procedures and a schedule for notifying the chosen team members.
    3.2.2. Notify the team members on a need-to-know basis. If you have an internal suspect, be sure that no one who might be in cahoots with the suspect is allowed on the incident-response team. And, keep in mind that notifying human-resources personnel or too many people too early could cause the spread of enough information to allow the suspect to flee — thus hindering your investigation. To keep any potential suspect in the dark (especially one who hasn't been identified yet), limit the number of personnel involved in any investigation as much as possible.
    3.2.3. Decide whether the incident level necessitates calling external team members, including law-enforcement personnel. If so, decide when they should be called. Additionally, decide when and if the public should be notified — for example, by contacting the media.

3.3. Establish a chain of command and secure communication procedures for assembling the assigned team members as soon as an incident is reported.

    3.3.1. Assign a separate team leader for each incident.

    3.3.2. Document all communications, including:

        3.3.2.1. The team members who were assigned

        3.3.2.2. The team leader who was appointed

        3.3.2.3. The date and time of the incident and of all subsequent communications that relate to the investigation

        3.3.2.4. A description of the incident

        3.3.2.5. The names of the employees who were interviewed

        3.3.2.6. The evidence that was gathered and their locations

        3.3.2.7. The team's response to the incident

3.4. Establish a chain of custody procedures for gathered evidence.

4. Set up procedures for logging and evidence gathering.

    4.1. Be sure that logging and monitoring systems, including those for firewall and IDS logging, are enabled and active — and accessible only to system administrators.

    4.2. Regularly check that the logging systems are properly functioning and recording information.

    4.3. Establish procedures for interviewing the system administrators, managers, and users of any affected systems.

    4.4. Establish procedures for determining which systems have been affected and for gathering evidence from hard disks and logs.

    4.5. Make certain that all activities will be documented.

5. Set up training classes and drill schedules.

    5.1. Provide regular training classes for incident-response team members in which you review the response procedures.

    5.2. To sharpen the team for the real thing, conduct regular drills with mock attacks.

6. Establish backup and recovery procedures for all applications and data.
   6.1. These procedures will be covered in detail in Chapter 14, "Recovering from Disasters." For the purposes of incident response, however, just remember to use your earlier assessment to establish priorities for the procedures.

Putting Ongoing Attack-Detection Processes in Motion

Check for the following indicators of attacks that are either in progress or complete:

- Unusually high network activity, either in general or at an expectedly slow time
- A log that shows irregular activity, that has missing portions, or that has been deleted altogether
- Evidence of pornography
- An unusual or unrecognized file that is residing on any of your systems
- An alert that has been triggered by an IDS or an irregularity that has been noted in a firewall log
- Defacement of any of your Web pages
- Degraded system performance
- Orphaned accounts, particularly those with administrative privileges or privileges that have recently been escalated
- Bogus data that appears when someone displays your Web site or tries to retrieve information from a company database, file, or application
- An unusual or unknown application that tries to call out from the network

Stopping an Attack

To stop an attack, abide by the following outline:

1. Isolate the attacked system from the network.

1.1. Based on your earlier assessment, decide whether the system is mission critical or can be taken down immediately. If possible, disconnect the system from the network.

1.2. Manipulate switches and routers to reroute traffic around the system.

2. Use backed-up media or equipment that is not susceptible to being re-attacked, if available.

3. If you have suspects and they are insiders, remove them from the system. (Just as you isolate systems, you should isolate suspects.)

4. Keep the system running so that evidence can be preserved.

5. If the system is under attack from a virus or worm, and that system is already protected by your antivirus software, perform a complete system scan and quarantine the offending critter.

6. Activate your incident-response plan.

7. Document all activities and responses.

Preserving Evidence of the Attack

For your incident investigation, forensics analysis, and evidence gathering, avail yourself of the following outline:

1. Evidence types
   1.1. Host-based — gathered from the following components of the server or workstation itself:
      1.1.1. Files, documents, and e-mail messages that are stored on the system
      1.1.2. Internet-browser history and cookie files
      1.1.3. Server logs that reside on the host
      1.1.4. Entire hard disks (not just individual files)
      1.1.5. The physical surroundings, for evidence of tampering or for a sticky note that contains a password and that is attached to a computer, placed under a mouse pad, or otherwise located in the immediate vicinity
   1.2. Network-based — gathered in the following places from traffic on the network rather than from the system itself:
      1.2.1. IDS and firewall logs
      1.2.2. Sniffed network traffic

2. Evidence-gathering states
   2.1. Live-system
      2.1.1. If an attacked or suspect system is still running, leave it on because shutting the system down by normal means alters files, which can damage or delete vital evidence.
      2.1.2. While the system is powered on, gather data in the following manner:
         2.1.2.1. Make complete images (backups) of the hard disks, using any commonly available system-backup utility or forensics tool.
         2.1.2.2. Capture as much information as possible about system activity, running processes, and memory contents. Dump everything into a file for later review.
         2.1.2.3. Map network connections to see what is connected to the system, and look for live processes that are attempting to make outbound network connections.
      2.1.3. If a system needs to be shut down, pull the plug. Although this act defies your education about how to turn off a computer, it can prevent the loss of volatile computer data during an investigation.
   2.2. Powered-down-system
      2.2.1. As with the live-system state, completely back up the compromised hard disks and store the originals away.
         2.2.1.1. Take advantage of the copies for investigation, and save the originals to use as evidence in court.
         2.2.1.2. Follow your rules for the chain of custody, and mark each drive with the following information:
            2.2.1.2.1. Date, time, and location when seized
            2.2.1.2.2. Description of contents
            2.2.1.2.3. Case number

2.2.2. Keep a complete record of all individuals that handle the evidence and when.

2.2.3. Seal each marked drive in a container or large envelope, and store it in a safe location that is designated as an evidence "warehouse."

2.2.4. Using forensics tools, review the following by looking at the disk copies:

2.2.4.1. The file systems and their structures

2.2.4.2. The files themselves and their contents

2.2.4.3. The deleted files

2.2.4.4. The hidden and encrypted files

2.2.4.5. Any keyword searches

Notifying the Appropriate Parties of the Attack

By the time that you have reached this stage, the relevant members of your incident-response team have long been notified. To determine who among management personnel, law-enforcement authorities, and the public should be notified next and when, follow your incident-response plan.

Taking Corrective Action

After all is said and done, the culprits have been stopped or apprehended, and the system is secure again, complete the items that the following post-incident checklist contains:

1. Report the details of the incident to management personnel.

   1.1. What happened and when, and who was involved

   1.2. How it happened

   1.3. How it could have been prevented

2. Determine whether your IT security policy should be updated to prevent similar incidents in the future.

3. Review your firewall rules and other hardware settings to see how you can further harden all your systems.

4. Reconstruct the affected computers so that they can be put back online.

 Important

So, you finally tracked down the villain who caused you grief by taking down your network. However, cybervigilantism, which might be on your mind, can create additional problems just like its real-world counterpart can. It won't protect your network and, in fact, it could boomerang. Furthermore, if the attack was launched from a third-party server, your counterattack could harm innocent people. Hack backs are not a good idea.

CHAPTER 14

RECOVERING FROM DISASTERS

AFTER A DISASTER OCCURS, YOU NEED TO IMPLE-
ment a recovery plan. Regardless of the cause of the disaster — a
hack attack or a natural catastrophe, such as a flood or lightning
strike — the computer will be out of service and disrupting your
business processes.

Maintaining backups of clean applications and of recent data
provides the best defense against disasters. Doing so means that no
matter what happens to your hardware, your software is restorable.
A good approach is thinking of your systems as machine-less. Sound
too far out? Maybe. But, if the heart of each system — the heart con-
sisting of the applications and the data — is portable and copied
somewhere else, it won't be lost to the whims of people or of
nature. Don't become emotionally attached, or married, to your IT
systems. They are only machines, and machines don't get married —
people do. Think beyond the machines and take your systems to
another level.

Tip

> Countless types of disasters exist that could strike your facilities and affect your systems. The best blanket contingency is maintaining the safety of your backups and planning for your recovery, rather than focusing on the tragic possibilities. Of course, if your area is prone to a particular disaster type, such as hurricanes or earthquakes, plan for them accordingly.

To implement a successful disaster-recovery program, perform the following steps:

1. Conduct a business impact analysis (BIA).
2. Schedule regular backups.
3. Store your backups in safe locations, including off-site ones.
4. Develop a recovery plan.

To conduct a BIA, perform the following steps:

1. Identify your most critical business systems — IT or otherwise — in a similar manner as that described in Chapter 3, "Assessing Your System."
2. Determine the impact that any catastrophic loss would have on those systems.
3. Attach a financial cost to the loss of the systems.
4. Rank and prioritize the systems in order of importance.

To schedule regular backups, perform the following steps:

1. Be aware of the types of backups:
   1.1. Full — All the data on a particular system is backed up.
   1.2. Incremental — Only the data that has been modified since a given date and time is backed up.
   1.3. Delta — Only the changes that have been made to data since the previous backup are backed up (which means that unmodified data is never backed up).
2. Base the type and frequency of your backups on the results of your BIA.

To store your backups in safe locations, abide by the following outline:

1. Note that backups can be manual or automatic.
   1.1. Enterprise systems necessitate automatic backups.
   1.2. Manual backups are adequate only for home users.
2. Be aware that automatic backups come in two varieties:
   2.1. Batch jobs that run at regular intervals
   2.2. Live systems that back up data as that data is being written to disk or another storage medium
      2.2.1. Redundant array of independent disks (RAID) systems
      2.2.2. Storage area networks (SANs)
      2.2.3. Remote journaling
3. If possible, create multiple backups and securely store one of them off site.
   3.1. At least 25 miles away, or far enough away from disasters that are common to the area of your facility
4. To enjoy the best situation, arrange for all of your data to be mirrored in an identical facility that is located remotely. Such a failover facility is an exact replica of your original facility. It contains identical equipment and data as the original; if a breakdown occurs at the original facility, the systems automatically switch to those at the failover facility. Such switching is transparent to users who simply see the systems running without missing a beat. However, failover facilities are costly so they are best used for large enterprises and, even then, only for mission-critical systems and data.

To develop a recovery plan, abide by the following outline:

1. Based on the BIA, develop the recovery plan with business units and IT departments.
2. Keep in mind that the first goal of any recovery plan is the protection of human life. Be sure that everyone will be safely brought out from a disaster scenario.

3. Assign responsibilities to individual coordinators of teams within departments. Clearly define the scope of their responsibilities and activities.

4. Be sure that personnel will be trained and that dry runs of the plan will be conducted at least annually.

5. Plan for alternate facilities.

    5.1 Hot — A fully equipped facility that is ready to go when disaster strikes

    5.2 Warm — A partially equipped facility that can be staffed but not immediately run at the time of disaster

    5.3. Cold — An empty facility that needs to be equipped and staffed at the time of disaster

6. If you will be using a third-party location, make certain of the following:

    6.1. The other party will allow you to use their facility for whatever activity you need conducted there.

    6.2. The other party supports your recovery plan. A misunderstanding can ruin your plan during the active disaster.

    6.3. The facility is fully equipped to handle your operation and has been thoroughly inspected during the BIA.

Chapter 15

Securing Your Wireless Network

AS WIRELESS ACCESS BECOMES MORE POPULAR
and convenient, it also generates the largest holes in existing company
networks. In fact, wireless access can turn into the open back door
of an otherwise extremely secure network.

On the one hand, companies are taking up the habit of establishing and using wireless networks — especially when saving money
is involved — as the people in charge discover how easy it is to do
so. On the other hand, wireless usage within a company should be
strictly delineated in the IT security policy and closely watched after
that. To begin with, all wireless network traffic should be encrypted.
So, set up a virtual private network (VPN), which is essentially a
private tunnel on a public network, for your wireless traffic. Plenty
of software packages — both free and proprietary — are available
that will make your wireless traffic private and secure.

At that point, all users should be allowed to use only wireless
access points (WAPs) that are connected to the corporate VPN. Otherwise, a user could circumvent your firewall just as he or she could
through an unauthorized modem on your network. In other words,
by using a workstation on the network that has a WAP directly connected to the Internet, a user could bring in malicious code and then
inadvertently transfer that code to the corporate network.

Here are some rules for securing your wireless network:

- Change the default settings and passwords on all WAPs. The factory defaults are known in the hacker world and available on the Internet.

- Change the service set identifier (SSID) that is set by default on all WAPs. Because the SSID uniquely names your wireless network, don't select one that would give away your identity (just as you wouldn't select a password that would do so). For example, choose *network* rather than the name of your company. Better yet, disable the SSID broadcast feature on your WAPs, if possible, so that anyone who tries to connect to your WAPs will see only a blank name displayed.

- Place each WAP in the center of an office, even though a WAP that is placed near a window can more easily detect a signal. Because most WAPs are short range, placing one near the center of a room will cause the signal to fade before it leaves the room.

- Enable Wired Equivalent Privacy (WEP) encryption. You might be thinking that WEP encryption is weak and easy to crack and that, furthermore, tools to do so are freely available on the Internet. However, to someone who is wandering around the neighborhood with a laptop containing a wireless card, the presence of WEP encryption could be enough to cause that person to move on to the next WAP.

- Turn off a WAP when it is not in use. A WAP that is turned off can't receive signals and thus can't be broken into.

- Obtain the latest firmware upgrades — which might contain security patches — for your WAPs.

- Perform your own audits. Download Netstumbler or Kismet from the Internet, and drive around your office to see whether you can connect to a WAP.

- Segregate your wireless network from your wired network. Create a setup in which the WAPs provide the only direct connection to the Internet, and route all traffic through a switch, a firewall, or a router that uses Network Address Translation (NAT).

- Enable Media Access Control (MAC) address filtering and disable the Dynamic Host Configuration Protocol (DHCP) on each WAP, if possible. Doing the former means that only computers having the MAC addresses allowed by the filter will be able to connect to the WAP. Doing the latter means that wireless intruders will not be able to connect to the WAP without a static IP address. Sure, MAC addresses can be spoofed and static IP addresses can be scanned or sniffed, but such activities are not for the amateur.

- If you do disable DHCP, use hard-to-guess and nonsequential IP addresses on the network. Although hackers know the limited ranges of unroutable IP addresses that are assigned to most routers, and they can scan or guess the addresses that are in use, this small roadblock may be enough to throw off an intruder.

Of the previous rules, the most important for securing your wireless network are the following:

- Change the SSID and, if possible, disable the SSID broadcast feature.
- Enable WEP encryption.
- Enable MAC address filtering.

CHAPTER 16

WRITING SECURE PROGRAMMING CODE

BECAUSE PROGRAMMING CODE ACTS AS THE heart of everything that a computer does, writing code that is secure is an essential part of the overall security process. So, why is secure coding overlooked so often — and why does this chapter appear so late in this book? The main reason is that coding in general has faded into the background in the minds of many IT professionals — who don't have the same job description as software developers do. Because the code works behind the scenes, it seems mysterious and too complicated for outsiders, so it is more easily forgotten than not.

Many of the details about how to write secure code are beyond the scope of this book, and a large number of volumes exist on this subject alone. The point of this chapter is to provide a checklist of the items that every software-development team should follow to facilitate the IT security effort.

Note

A nice reference for healthy programming practices is *Secure Coding: Principles & Practices,* Mark G. Graff and Kenneth R. van Wyk (O'Reilly, 2003). This little book — just 224 pages — provides checklists of best practices, checklists of things to avoid, case studies, and descriptions of how to integrate the whole security picture into the software-development life cycle.

To write secure code, you should first be aware of the following major categories of code flaws:

- Invalid input — data containing certain characters that a user feeds to the application (which occurs either directly on the command line or when the Web browser appends that data to the URL). The Web server sends this dessert from the end of the URL meal to be digested by a database server or back-end application. However, SQL and other server commands as well as certain innocuous-looking characters (**&**, **!**, **#**, **$**, **%**, *****, **@**) cause server indigestion. These characters, either by themselves or in combination with commands, can kick off unwanted processes, access databases, or bypass authentication. They should always be stripped out by the application.

- Buffer overruns — the result of trying to cram too much data into the memory space allocated to the application for input. The effect is that the memory immediately following the buffer is overwritten. In a best-case scenario, the application crashes. In a worst-case scenario, the overflowed data directly accesses another application in memory — which allows a malicious user to gain access to the computer. Any extra data should be kicked out by the application.

- Exposed information — critical data that is hard-coded in the application's source code or a Web page's HTML code (both of which users can see or access). All user IDs and passwords should be stored in encrypted authentication systems on servers that are separate from the main application server.

System and other vital information that is necessary for the
ongoing maintenance of the application should be stored in
documentation that is inaccessible to users. Again, the information should be stored on a different server than the ones
that contain the application and Web site.

Next, you should adhere to the following basic rules for writing
secure code:

1. Learn about the flaws in your programming language and adapt
   to them.
   1.1. Base the choice of programming language on the needs of
        the project, rather than on security grounds. After the choice
        has been made, however, you must build security into the
        development effort.
   1.2. Take advantage of any built-in security features that the lan-
        guage boasts.
   1.3. Become conversant with known flaws and vulnerabilities of
        the language and with existing workarounds.
   1.4. When workarounds don't exist, create them.

2. Incorporate security into the application-development life cycle.
   2.1. Make security one of the initial requirements.
   2.2. Include security planning in the architectural design.
   2.3. At every stage in the life cycle, check the progress of secu-
        rity implementation.
   2.4. At the end of each development cycle, apply regression
        testing to the code and review the code for security defects.

3. Frequently review the code for security defects, and remove
   developers' back doors when they are no longer needed.
   3.1. During code reviews, check for the major flaws that were
        previously listed.
   3.2. Note that developers frequently write code with shortcuts
        that allow them to bypass authentication and access con-
        trols, so they can complete their work and meet deadlines.
        Double check that these back doors have been removed
        when they are no longer needed — no matter how early in
        the development cycle it is.

To Automatically Check Buffer Overruns or Not to Check: C vs. Java

Two very different languages — C and Java — provide an interesting comparison. The C language is notorious for allowing buffer overruns because the compiler doesn't check the bounds of your arrays. It can therefore be a hacker's toy. But, C is fast and lightweight (which means that it requires less code than other languages to do a job), and it provides direct access to memory. All of these characteristics make it a great language for developing device drivers and other low-level applications that directly control the computer.

Java, on the other hand, is the enterprise world's Goliath. As a language that easily performs all the heavy-duty processing required by enterprise systems and applications, Java is the darling of developers that create Web and networking applications. Furthermore, Java is fast and cross-platform, and it automatically checks the bounds of arrays but does not provide direct access to memory — so it can't get into trouble. However, a Java application can still take malicious input from a user and pass it along to your system. Plus, hostile Java applets, which are bits of code embedded in Web pages that add functionality, can wreak just as much havoc as full Java applications can.

When deciding which language to use, keep in mind that using Java to write a device driver, for example, is like using a sledge hammer to perform delicate surgery. Alternatively, you could easily make your C program more secure by writing bounds-checking code into it. Choose your language first and then build security into it.

4. Maintain separate development, testing, and production environments.
    4.1. If space permits, assign each environment its own server.
    4.2. Move code from one environment to another only by using established deployment schedules and procedures — and then only in a hierarchical sequence from development to testing to production.

5. Make production code inaccessible to developers.
    5.1. Move only fully tested and reviewed code from testing to production, and allow only system administrators or IT staff (who should be the only ones with access rights to production servers) to do so.
    5.2. After the code is in production, allow no one other than the staff just mentioned to have access to it.
    5.3. Make certain that all updates and modifications to production code occur through established change-control procedures.

Finally, be aware of the following details regarding the major code flaws:

1. Invalid input
    1.1. Note that any parameter that is passed to an application can contain executable code, so such a parameter can be an attack source.
    1.2. Do not trust any input, including the following:
        1.2.1. A URL that has been passed from a Web site
        1.2.2. Data that was entered into a form on a Web site
        1.2.3. The name of a file that is passed as a parameter
        1.2.4. Any command-line parameter
        1.2.5. Any SQL query string
    1.3. In the application code, validate all input against known vulnerabilities of the servers or workstations that the code will be running on.
    1.4. Note that validation can consist of the following:
        1.4.1. Conditional statements that block undesired parameters
        1.4.2. Matching against patterns, such as regular expressions
        1.4.3. Using an external configuration file or an XML file to test for valid input

2. Buffer overruns
    2.1. Set predefined buffer sizes by setting array sizes and variable bounds.
    2.2. If the size of the input is greater than the size of the buffer, exit the application.

3. Exposed information
   3.1. Display only generic error messages because actual messages and stack traces contain information that can be valuable to hackers. A Web application should redirect to a generic error page; a client application should display a nondescript dialog box. The generic message should say only that there was a technical problem and optionally provide a phone number for contacting technical support. After the message is displayed, the application should terminate.
   3.2. Never place unencrypted or clear-text passwords in source code. Always place passwords in files that are external to the application, and be sure that the passwords are encrypted and accessible only to administrators. Better yet, use separate authentication servers, such as LDAP servers.

CHAPTER 17

SECURING WINDOWS, UNIX, AND LINUX

THE WINDOWS AND UNIX OPERATING SYSTEMS each have their own peculiarities and unique security holes. Linux belongs to the Unix family so, for the most part, its security issues correspond to those of the Unix system. However, Linux does have a few features that differ from those of Unix.

Security problems that affect Windows are publicized far more than those that affect Unix or Linux, but the Unix twins possess their share of serious vulnerabilities. So, why does Windows take it on the chin? Partly, it does deserve its reputation for being weaker regarding security. Windows was designed for ease of use rather than for remaining secure — which is something that hackers are fully aware of. However, you need to view the weaknesses of Windows with a certain amount of perspective.

First, Windows is less expensive and more ubiquitous than Unix. (Sure, Linux is free, but more on that in a moment.) Because Windows can be easily purchased and then installed anywhere, it can be found on over 95 percent of the workstations and desktops in existence. Unix, on the other hand, is usually reserved for corporate and university back-end systems, and it requires users to have shell accounts to access these systems. The bottom line is that Windows boasts a healthy portion of the corporate LAN market, whereas Unix remains in the data center.

Second, Windows includes a well-documented, easy-to-use application programming interface (API) that can complete everything from handy programming tasks to system-administration tasks — such as copying and deleting an entire hard disk, which is something that hackers salivate over. The API can spoof e-mail messages, open and close dialog boxes, run remote commands, create new file shares, and take over your entire system — and this list provides just a tiny hint of the many toys that are available to legitimate users and hackers alike. In addition to countless independent Web sites that contain API information from Windows fans worldwide, Microsoft provides an online guidebook to it all on its own Web site.

Third, although Unix contains gaping holes just like Windows does, its cost and inaccessibility make it a harder target for outside hackers to attack. Furthermore, Unix has two decades on Windows, so many of its vulnerabilities are well known and taught early on to any aspiring system administrator.

At this point, you're probably saying, what about Linux? It's free and even easier to get than Windows is because you can download it directly from any Linux distribution site. As a result, Linux can't claim immunity to attacks; it suffers its share of buffer-overrun problems and other code vulnerabilities and has recently exhibited some serious kernel flaws. However, hackers haven't victimized Linux as much as they have Windows, and viruses seem to be a Windows problem that rarely affect Linux. What is the reason for this relatively protected status?

Once again, it's partly because Windows holds the predominant market share. Although Linux has been heavily publicized because of its rapid growth in the server market, it possesses only an infinitesimal share of the desktop market. (Linux thus poses a greater threat to the related and more costly Unix systems.) The media has puffed Linux up when the truth is that, like Unix, it isn't as ubiquitous as Windows is (which could change in the future, however).

Two more reasons for the lesser victimization of Linux might be "honor among thieves" and "not biting the hand that feeds you." After all, the best hacking tools are designed for Linux systems. However, it's more likely that Linux does enjoy a security edge over its Windows counterpart. The current distributions include packet-filtering firewalls as standard features that are built in to the kernel and that are turned on by default during the installation of the operating system. Windows XP, which is the latest Windows incarnation, is the first in its family to include an equivalent client-side firewall. And, only recently has Windows XP Service Pack 2 (SP2) included a firewall that is turned on by default.

Despite their security differences, all three operating systems experience their trials and tribulations in the following general areas:

- File sharing
- Open ports and unnecessary services
- Permissions and accounts
- Patching and updating

While sharing the same general security-problem areas, the different systems express specific issues within those areas differently — requiring you to take different actions to secure your Windows, Unix, or Linux system.

Closing the Holes: File Sharing

To close the holes in your Windows system that are created by file sharing, perform the following actions:

- Disable File and Printer Sharing unless it is absolutely needed. Definitely disable it on any server that is not a file server, such as a DNS, HTTP, SMTP, or other application server.
- Disable NetBIOS over TCP/IP unless it is needed to connect a Windows 2000 or later system to a Windows 95 or Windows 98 one. Stick with TCP/IP only, even for your network shares. TCP/IP contains numerous flaws — NetBIOS contains more.

Tip

If possible, migrate up from Windows 95 and Windows 98 — because they possess no security whatsoever. Unlike Windows NT and later systems, which use the NTFS file system that allows for file-system and more-granular security, Windows 95 and Windows 98 possess no granularity at all. A user can bypass any password system simply by canceling the logon screen or by rebooting into MS-DOS, which is an equally insecure system. Windows 98 has reached the end of its life cycle — a good excuse for replacing it.

- Make certain that any system with File and Printer Sharing is not directly connected to the Internet. Place systems that require shares behind routers that use Network Address Translation (NAT) or behind hardware firewalls.
- Make shares password protected. Although hackers can still invade such shares by using password-cracking utilities, access is more difficult.
- To prevent someone from outside the network attempting to access file shares, block ports 135 and 139, which are the file-sharing ports, at the router.
- Disable or remove the default administrator shares — which are the infamous IPC$ and C$ shares. Access to these shares compromises the entire system, and if used to hopscotch to another computer in the workgroup, domain, or subnet, access compromises the entire network segment.

To close the holes in your Unix or Linux system that are created by file sharing, perform the following actions:

- Disable Network File System (NFS), which is the Unix and Linux equivalent of File and Printer Sharing, unless it is absolutely needed. On a server that isn't a file server, the same rule as that for Windows applies: turn off NFS.
- If NFS is required on a limited basis, make the shares read-only and block write access.

- If you have a mixed network (meaning that Windows and Linux servers are cohabiting), use Samba according to the same rules. Keep in mind that a Linux-based computer running Samba but connected to an insecure Windows-based computer is equivalent to an open door.

Closing the Holes: Open Ports and Unnecessary Services

To close the holes in your Windows system that are created by open ports and unnecessary services, perform the following actions:

1. To close ports and filter services, use Internet Protocol Security (IPsec) and IP filtering. If your system is not Windows XP, install a host-based firewall. (Windows XP has a firewall that is turned on by default. Keep it on.)

2. If you don't need the following services (which allow remote access to the system and might already be turned on by default), disable them but don't remove them (in case you need to turn them on later under restricted circumstances):
    2.1. Remote Procedure Call Service (used by Blaster and other perimeter worms)
    2.2. Remote Registry Service
    2.3. Telnet and FTP
    2.4. Messenger Service and Alerter Service
    2.5. ClipBook Service
    2.6. Remote Desktop Service and Terminal Services
    2.7. IP Forwarding Service
    2.8. Internet Information Services (IIS)

   To close the holes in your Unix or Linux system that are created by open ports and unnecessary services, perform the following actions:

1. Use the netstat command to check whether any open ports are running services.

2. Turn off unneeded services in startup scripts (which reside in /etc/rc.d, /etc/init.d, or similar directories) by commenting them

out in the scripts. Note that the services in these scripts are started when the system is started; if they are not needed at that time, consider them unneeded.

3. When access to the TCP services that are controlled by xinetd is by IP address, service type, or both, use TCP wrappers to block that access. (The xinetd service is a master service that was created for the single control of FTP, Telnet, Finger, and so on.)

4. Use host-based packet-filtering firewalls (which are now standard on Linux), such as iptables, to block unneeded and unwanted service requests.

5. Disable source routing by making sure that internal network IP addresses are not exposed to outside networks or the Internet.

6. Disable the following services, their ports, and any banners that contain their service names or version information (or restrict these items to the bare minimum that is required):

   6.1. All 'r' service that are used to allow remotely logging on or connecting

   6.2. ICMP requests

   6.3. DNS zone transfers (which you disable by blocking inbound requests on TCP port 53 or by restricting that port's access to secondary DNS servers in the network that belong to the zone)

   6.4. FTP (port 21)

   6.5. Telnet (port 23)

   6.6. EXPN and VRFY through SMTP (port 25)

   6.7. Finger (port 79)

   6.8. portmapper and RPC (port 111)

   6.9. X server (port 6000), which can be used to open a remote shell on the desktop

Note

When you disable DNS zone transfers, take care that you don't restrict or block UDP port 53 — which is needed to use DNS. If you close the UDP port, DNS lookups will be blocked. TCP port 53 is the one that is used for zone transfers.

Closing the Holes: Permissions and Accounts

To close the holes in your Windows system that are created by permissions and accounts, perform the following actions:

- To maintain consistent security policies for users across domains, remove any domain trust relationships that are not necessary. In Windows 2000, Windows Server 2003, and Windows XP, use Group Policy settings.

- Review all groups and accounts and restrict their administrative access as much as possible. Admin privileges can creep into some groups because adding a user that has these privileges to a group spreads them to the entire group. You should also restrict accounts that have domain-wide access.

- Rename the Administrator account, and restrict all types of guest accounts (accounts that have Everyone access). On IIS, make sure to set the IUSR account (a type of guest account that allows people to see the Web site hosted on the server) to read-only.

- For operating-system files and folders and for registry files, allow full control only to the Administrator and System accounts. For all other users, disable access to these files or set them to read-only.

- Create partitions or use multiple disk drives. Set up each partition or disk drive with the NTFS file system, and use one partition or drive to store the operating system, another to store application software, and yet another to store data. This setup enhances security but can slow performance, so plan carefully before you implement it.

- In Windows Explorer, select Folder Options from the Tools menu, click the View tab, and make sure that **Hide extensions for known file types** is not selected. Doing so can help you identify viruses and worms that have the .vbs file name extension, which identifies files that are written in the VBScript scripting language. Viruses and worms that target Windows are often written in this language because VBScript code runs only on Windows. If all file name extensions remain hidden, a virus that is named Somevirus.txt.vbs, for example, will appear in Windows Explorer as Somevirus.txt — thus masquerading as an innocent text file.

- Hide any Security Accounts Manager (SAM), LanMan hash, or other account-password files, or make them inaccessible.
- Periodically audit all accounts and groups and remove any stale or inactive ones.

To close the holes in your Unix or Linux system that are created by permissions and accounts, perform the following actions:

- Review users and groups and remove SUID and GUID access to files where that access is not necessary.
- Restrict root access to only the local console, and check that only one superuser account plus at least one regular user account exists.
- See that IT personnel avoid logging on as root. This account has unrestricted access to system files and directories, and it does not receive a warning when anything that is vital to system functioning is about to be accidentally deleted. Instead, a system administrator should log on as a regular user and, when necessary, use the su command to switch to root-level access.
- Take care that the $PATH environment variable points only to system directories and has no dot (.) defined.
- For system directories, grant full access to only the root account and grant read-only access to all other users.
- Use chroot to hide the server's root path and confine users to their own, private paths. (You can also use chroot on Apache Web servers to segregate the Web server's root directory from that of the host server.)

Note

Windows has a very different file-permission system from that of the Unix and Linux family. This crucial distinction is important for securing these operating systems. The administrator role of Windows differs from the root account of Unix in its privilege levels. Furthermore, Windows makes use of domain controllers and Microsoft Active Directory, whereas Unix relies on a different domain-mapping system altogether.

Closing the Holes: Patching and Updating

To close the holes in your Windows system that are created by patching and updating (or the lack thereof), perform the following actions:

1. Make certain that you are running the latest version of Windows. Furthermore, review the most recent upgrades and services packs for that version to determine which ones are needed for your particular system configuration.

2. Enable and use Windows Update, but set it to alert you when updates and patches become available, rather than to automatically install them. You can then review the updates before installing them, thus avoiding buggy and unnecessary downloads.

3. Take special care to keep current on patches and security alerts for the following applications, which have had more than their share of problems and holes:
   3.1. Outlook
   3.2. Internet Explorer
   3.3. Internet Information Services (IIS)

To close the holes in your Unix or Linux system that are created by patching and updating (or the lack thereof), perform the following actions:

1. Subscribe to the updating service for your particular distribution. The service will notify you every time an update becomes available, by displaying a flashing icon on your desktop or by sending you an e-mail alert.

2. Check that the latest version of the kernel for your distribution is installed.

3. Before installing any patch, security update, or other download, use md5sum to check its integrity against its MD5 signature. If the download doesn't pass the md5sum muster, immediately delete it from the system and download it again. And, if an MD5 signature is not available, don't download and don't install.

4. Take special care to keep current on patches and security alerts for the following applications, which have had more than their share of problems and holes:
   4.1. Apache Web server
   4.2. sendmail

CHAPTER 18

PROTECTING PRIVACY, PREVENTING IDENTITY THEFT, AND PROTECTING CHILDREN

FOLLOWING THE GUIDELINES THAT THIS BOOK has outlined up to now should protect the privacy of your customers and your staff and prevent the theft of their identities. Nevertheless, you should make your staff aware of how to generally protect themselves and your company's customers. Staff members can fall prey to scams when accessing Web sites from the office because business Web sites sometimes ask for personal information that identity thieves can use. Furthermore, a clever social engineer can breach the company's firewall which, in any case, doesn't protect against e-mail attachments that contain password-stealing trojans directed at individual employees. Some staff members might also have access to confidential customer lists that include detailed contact information. And, when training your staff how to compute safely, it's a good idea to include points about how to protect children in the home-computing environment. Although the latter are not business issues, they will be of interest to staff members that have children and home computers.

To protect privacy and prevent identity theft, train your staff to do the following:

1. Follow the rules that were outlined in Chapter 8, "Securing E-mail."

2. Never provide your social security number or that of anyone else in an online environment. If the number is absolutely required, look for the following to confirm that the Web site uses Secure Sockets Layer (SSL), which encrypts the transaction so that sniffers cannot read it:

   2.1. The URL begins with **https://** rather than **http://**.

   2.2. The browser displays a small lock icon in the lower-right corner. (Note that some browsers display this icon, some don't, and some provide the option to display it.)

3. Subscribe to as few online newsletters as possible and avoid signing up for online offers, especially if they are not work related. If an opt-out feature for online requests or marketing messages exists, avail yourself of it.

4. When you set up the profile for a new e-mail account, enter the minimum amount of detail that the e-mail application requires. Don't volunteer additional information or boast about achievements, which just add fuel to a thief's fire.

5. Use aliases when you make postings to newsgroups. Subscribe only to newsgroups that are business related and mask your identity by using different e-mail addresses.

6. On your own time, periodically check your credit reports and online public records to see what is available to the public.

   6.1. Do some private-detective work on yourself.

   6.2. If your last name is unique, use Google to search for the name. The results could be interesting: Did you once post embarrassing comments to a newsgroup that you would now rather forget? Those comments might still show up.

6.3. Regularly check public records and online "people-finding" services to see what is posted about you. Wherever possible, request removal from the online versions of these records or, at the very least, that access be allowed only with a password.

7. Never respond to an e-mail message from any company that requests your name, address, and social security number. Only a few companies ask for social security numbers online, but they are in the minority. When in doubt, verify by using that ancient technology called the telephone.

8. Never reply to spam — even to offers that are directly related to your work — and don't respond to offers to be taken off the senders' mailing lists.

9. Before you throw out any items that contain names, addresses, or social security numbers, shred the items as described in Chapter 5, "Taking Care of Physical Security." (At home, these items include old telephone and utility bills as well as any other bills that contain personal information.)

To protect children, train your staff to do the following:

- Talk openly with your children about which Web sites and chat rooms they are visiting. Set clear boundaries about what you will and will not allow them to do online.
- Make certain that all e-mail accounts are subaccounts of yours so that you can set controls and passwords and supervise all of your children's activities.
- Use filtering software, such as Net Nanny or CYBERsitter, to block sites that contain pornographic, gambling, hate, or other objectionable information. Check the browser's history and cookie files to see which sites have been visited.
- Take advantage of features that allow you to set different access levels for blocking adult content. (America Online and MSN are two providers that offer such features.)
- Place your computers in areas that allow you to see all of your children's online activity, and restrict their access to times when you are present to supervise them. The best lock

is an eye: Don't allow your children to work on the computer out of sight.

- As your children become teenagers, they become more technically savvy and more difficult to supervise, so some of the previous guidelines may become impossible to enforce. The best approach at this age is communicating openly about online activity. Pay attention to general changes in behavior or to secretive online behavior. Impressionable young minds can be lured by sexual offers, and harmful strangers can pretend to be friends.

CHAPTER 19

TAKING A LOOK AT FUTURE TRENDS

THE SUGGESTIONS IN THIS BOOK COMPRISE THE safe computing practices that will stand the test of time. You can — and should — implement these practices despite any changes that occur in hardware or software technology.

However, the world of security does not stand still. It continues to be a cat-and-mouse game between attackers and their victims: attackers attacking, their victims recovering and then fixing, and the attackers returning with fresh ways to attack. Although the circle never closes, some security is always better than no security at all. Even an imperfect patch can provide just enough protection to deter a wandering hacker.

Given these facts, here are some trends in computer security for you to be watching out for:

- Virus-attack and worm-attack cycles are shortening.

  The amount of time between a vulnerability being discovered and a virus becoming available that exploits that vulnerability is decreasing — so much so that as soon as a hole is found, a malicious coder somewhere in the world will post a hacking tool to the Internet within minutes. These people, like legitimate developers, hone their skills by building upon previous viral adventures and by making them more lethal. Zero-day attacks, in which fresh exploits hit the wires before any defensive measures can be taken, have already emerged.

- Malware authors will still be up to the same old tricks.

  Despite advances in programming technology, mass-mailing worms such as Mydoom will still be effective. For this reason, old-fashioned safe e-mail practices will remain important. Until users learn to stop clicking unsolicited e-mail attachments from strangers, these tricks will continue.

- Hackers will instigate virus and worm attacks to make money, not simply to show off or vandalize a Web site.

  The day of the smart-aleck teenager writing virus and worm code in his or her basement is rapidly becoming extinct. Writing such code is instead becoming a pursuit of organized-crime outfits that are located outside the United States — specifically, in Russia, China, Brazil, Korea, and Eastern Europe. These gangsters are teaming up with errant programmers to spread spam (mostly through viruses), build phishing Web sites, and break into databases to steal identities and credit-card numbers. Identity thieves that operate in criminal rings on rogue Web sites openly trade personal information. The idea of hacking as a "techno-thrill" for precocious teenagers that discover new cyberfrontiers and then vandalize is over. Hacking is now big business: It's about stolen identities and credit-card numbers for sale on the black market by criminal gangs.

- Application-level attacks will become more frequent than network-level attacks.

  As more-protective hardware is installed and networks become more challenging to crack, attacks will more likely be in the form of malicious application code that can slip through router restrictions and firewall rules, rather than code that attacks the routers and firewalls themselves. Malicious code will thus continue to hide on Web sites and piggyback on e-mail messages.

- Attacks will target e-commerce Web sites and become more complex to do so.

  Since attacks are now about money, and the money lies in e-commerce, that is where the criminals will go. Defacing the mom-and-pop Web site for fun is no longer where the action is. The gangs will continue to hit big banks and major e-commerce sites and to hunt for other big game. Spyware, which consists of code that is automatically downloaded (in the background) to a client visiting a Web site, will continue to proliferate — but with the potential for hiding viruses, trojans, and worms. Spyware is ostensibly used by legitimate companies to track their users' Web habits for the purposes of marketing research. However, less-savory Web sites can use spyware for more malicious purposes.

- Internet service providers (ISPs) will become more active in the defense of their gateways.

  After the Blaster worm was let loose, more ISPs began to take control of securing their network connections to their customers. Before, many ISPs provided antivirus software on their servers, but now many routinely block open ports, such as the one that is used for Windows shares (port 139), to stop the most egregious abuses of their networks. Furthermore, protection through the signatures that are required for antivirus software may eventually move upstream to the ISPs. The reason is that as the number of viruses rapidly increases, the sheer number of required signatures could overwhelm their ability to be updated. ISPs can also be expected to do more to combat spam, and many are already working hard at that.

- As a standard feature on all workstations, firewalls will be installed in addition to antivirus software.

  All computers will come with both antivirus software and firewall software installed. On a similar note, security suites for computer hosts that contain antivirus and firewall software as well as spyware detection and removal tools have recently hit the market.

- A license might be required to gain access to networks — including the Internet.

  This idea requires everyone to provide some sort of digital identification to access the Internet or log on to an individual network. Some people say that such a requirement would stop identify theft and spam because individuals attempting such hacks would have to identify themselves to even get on to the Internet or network. One possible implementation is a secure chip that comes embedded in every new computer and that uniquely identifies that computer. Only those individuals that have the correct chip would be given permission to access the Internet or network.

- The perimeter in perimeter defense is dissolving.

  As companies integrate their business partners and outsourcing vendors into their networks, the definition of the network perimeter becomes blurred. The definition is further complicated by firewall architectures that are segmented to grant access to these external users. The old demarcation between those who are inside the network and those who are outside no longer applies.

- Wireless access and wireless devices break the perimeter even more.

  Wireless access points, which can already bypass the perimeter altogether, make up only part of the problem. The growth of other wireless devices — cell phones, radio frequency identification (RFID) tags, BlackBerry devices, and personal digital assistants (PDAs) — that directly access corporate networks makes the problem worse.

- Passwords in their current form will become obsolete.

  Stealing and cracking user IDs and passwords has become easier than ever. It is especially easy for criminal gangs who drop keystroke loggers onto users' desktops through spyware,

viruses, and trojans. Two-factor authentication, which requires
a token that generates a one-time password, may become
the rage in authentication technology. To access high-risk
data, such as that involved in financial transactions, a user
would need to enter the one-time password plus a regular
user ID and password.

- Social engineering attacks will continue apace.

  Some things never change, and people are just as gullible as
  ever. In fact, as firewall and router technology improves, con
  games to steal user IDs, passwords, and corporate data will
  become the way to go. Phishing is one example of social
  engineering.

- Outsourcing will become a security issue.

  As more software-application development, consumer-loan
  servicing, and medical transcription move overseas, threats
  are created by placing exposed data in the hands of strangers
  who are not just outside the office but outside the country.
  Expect companies to impose strict quality and access controls
  on outsourced code and data. Such controls will be mandated
  both by plain old security considerations and by United States
  government regulations regarding privacy, such as the Health
  Insurance Portability and Accountability Act of 1996 (HIPAA)
  for medical information and the Gramm-Leach-Bliley Act for
  financial information.

Short Cheat Sheet for Computer Security

Four basic principles
- Install antivirus software.
- Use firewalls.
- Keep patches up-to-date.
- Select the users to grant access to.

Server-hardening rules
- Disable any unneeded services.
- Remove any unneeded accounts.
- Change the default settings.
- Restrict access.
- Segregate services onto individual servers.

Assessment

1. Catalog.
    1.1. Hardware
        1.1.1. Servers
        1.1.2. Workstations
        1.1.3. Networking equipment
    1.2. Software
        1.2.1. Developed in-house
        1.2.2. Purchased or outsourced
    1.3. Data
    1.4. Processes

2. Prioritize.

3. Evaluate.
    3.1. Values
    3.2. Potential threats

Policy

1. Plan for the policy to be:
    1.1. Accessible
    1.2. Understandable
    1.3. Segmented by department, function, or logical group
    1.4. Flexible and regularly updated

2. Implement the policy so that it includes:
    2.1. Approval by management
    2.2. The acceptable uses of hardware and software
    2.3. The hardware and software that is allowed
    2.4. An assignment of responsibilities for hardware and software installation and upgrades

Physical security

- Deal with the facility's location.
- Lock rooms and control access to facilities and systems.
- Secure equipment from theft and surveillance.

- Provide a single point of access.
- Use identification badges or systems.
- Destroy data and secure garbage.

Human resources

1. Hiring policies
   1.1. Screen and perform background checks prior to employment.
   1.2. Provide training during employment.

2. Termination procedures, including removal from systems

3. Defeating social engineers
   3.1. Verify all visitors and callers.
   3.2. Do not provide internal information to outsiders.

Software access controls

1. Putting software access controls in place
   1.1. Classify data.
   1.2. Create groups.
   1.3. Assign groups to classification levels.
   1.4. Choose authentication methods.
      1.4.1. Biometric solutions
      1.4.2. Cards or tokens
      1.4.3. Password systems

2. Password practices
   2.1. Increase password length.
   2.2. Do not use dictionary words nor personal information.
   2.3. Use a mixture of uppercase letters, lowercase letters, numbers, and characters.
   2.4. Never reveal nor write down a password.
   2.5. Limit the number of failed logon attempts.
   2.6. Set expiration dates and regularly change passwords.
   2.7. Enter a unique password for each system.
   2.8. Do not use password managers.
   2.9. Do not display filled-in logon screens.

E-mail

- Encrypt messages that contain passwords or other sensitive information.
- Use multiple e-mail accounts.
- When you receive a message, check whether you know the sender.
- Never reply to spam.
- Limit the distribution of your e-mail address.
- Never open unexpected or unrequested attachments.
- Ignore hoaxes and bogus security warnings.

Virus protection

- Install antivirus software on both workstations and servers.
- Regularly update the software.
- Keep patches up-to-date.
- Never open unrequested e-mail attachments.
- Scan all downloaded software.
- Restrict file sharing and network access.

Web-site security

- Restrict the information that is posted on your Web site.
- Segregate the Web application's root directory from the server's root directory.
- Validate input and mask sensitive URLs.
- Do not include sensitive information in client code.
- Harden Web servers like you do other network servers.

Perimeter defense

- Defense in depth
- Network segregation
- Firewall rules
- Intrusion detection

Intrusion detection

1. Overall strategy
    1.1. Complete a security audit.
    1.2. Conduct a penetration test.
    1.3. Install IDSs.
2. Hack attack cycle
    2.1. Scout the terrain.
    2.2. Plan the attack.
    2.3. Begin the attack.
    2.4. Escalate privileges.
    2.5. Leave a calling card.

Incident response

- Create an incident-response plan.
- Put attack-detection processes in motion.
- Stop an attack.
- Preserve evidence.
- Notify parties.
- Take corrective action.

Disaster recovery

- Conduct a business impact analysis (BIA).
- Schedule regular backups.
- Store your backups in safe locations, including offsite ones.
- Develop a recovery plan.

Wireless-network security

- Change the default settings and passwords on all WAPs.
- Change the SSID or make your WAPs anonymous.
- Place each WAP in the center of a room, away from windows.
- Enable WEP or other encryption.
- Segregate your wireless network from your wired network.
- Enable MAC address filtering and disable DHCP.

Secure coding

1. Major code flaws
    1.1. Invalid input
    1.2. Buffer overruns
    1.3. Exposed information

2. Basic rules
    2.1. Incorporate security into the application-development life cycle — as early as the initial-requirements phase.
    2.2. Frequently review code for security defects.
    2.3. Remove developers' back doors.
    2.4. Maintain separate development, testing, and production environments.

Windows, Unix, and Linux

1. Take special care to keep current on patches and security alerts for the following Windows applications:
    1.1. Outlook
    1.2. Internet Explorer
    1.3. Internet Information Server (IIS)

2. Take special care to keep current on patches and security alerts for the following Unix and Linux applications:
    2.1. Apache Web server
    2.2. sendmail

Web Sites to Check Daily

Table B.1

All-purpose computer-security sites

Site	Address
Internet Storm Center	*http://isc.sans.org*
SecurityTracker	*http://www.securitytracker.com*
CERT Coordination Center	*http://www.cert.org*
Astalavista Security Group	*http://www.astalavista.com*
Insecure.Org	*http://www.insecure.org*
SecurityFocus	*http://www.securityfocus.com*
Internet Security Systems	*http://www.iss.net*
eSecurity Planet	*http://www.esecurityplanet.com*
LinuxSecurity.com	*http://www.linuxsecurity.com*
Security News Portal	*http://www.securitynewsportal.com*
SearchSecurity.com	*http://searchsecurity.techtarget.com*
Security Pipeline	*http://informationweek.securitypipeline.com*

Table B.2
Virus-alert sites

Site	Address
Symantec	*http://www.symantec.com*
Sophos	*http://www.sophos.com*
Trend Micro	*http://www.trendmicro.com*
Panda Software	*http://www.pandasoftware.com*

TOOLS OF THE TRADE

Table C.1
All-purpose tools

All-purpose tool	Web site
Nessus	*http://www.nessus.org*
Netcat	*http://netcat.sourceforge.net*

Table C.2
Scanners

Scanner	Web site
Nmap	*http://www.insecure.org/nmap*
Nikto	*http://www.cirt.net/code/nikto.shtml*

Table C.3
Sniffers

Sniffer	Web site
Ethereal	*http://www.ethereal.com*
tcpdump	*http://www.tcpdump.org*
Ettercap	*http://ettercap.sourceforge.net*
Snort	*http://www.snort.org*

Table C.4
Password crackers

Password cracker	Web site
John the Ripper	*http://www.openwall.com/john*
LC (previously named L0phtCrack)	*http://www.atstake.com/products/lc*

Table C.5
Wireless tools

Wireless tool	Web site
Kismet	*http://www.kismetwireless.net*
NetStumbler	*http://www.stumbler.net*
AirSnort	*http://airsnort.shmoo.com*

Table C.6
Linux tool

Linux tool	Web site
chkrootkit	*http://www.chkrootkit.org*

Table C.7
Top 75 security tools

Top tools	Web site
List of favorite tools	*http://www.insecure.org/tools.html*

COMMON TCP PORTS

Table D.1

TCP services and their ports

TCP service	Port number
FTP	21
SSH	22
Telnet	23
SMTP	25
DNS	53
TFTP	69
Finger	79
HTTP	80
POP3	110
portmapper and Unix RPC	111
NetBIOS naming service	137
NetBIOS datagram service	139
IMAP	143
HTTPS	443
Unix X Windows	6000

THE TEN COMMANDMENTS OF COMPUTER SECURITY

1. Thou shalt know about social engineers and train thy people against them.
2. Thou shalt produce a clear and accessible security policy.
3. Thou shalt pay heed to physical security.
4. Thou shalt prudently hire employees and restrict information to outsiders.
5. Thou shalt maintain firm and defined access controls.
6. Thou shalt never reveal thy password nor make it easy to guess.
7. Thou shalt religiously patch and consistently update antivirus software.
8. Thou shalt harden thy servers and guard both the interior and the perimeter.
9. Thou shalt control remote access and carefully set up thy WAPs.
10. Thou shalt conduct regular backups, security audits, penetration tests, and code reviews.